SCIENCE AND THE BIBLE
Revised and Updated

SCIENCE AND THE BIBLE

by

HENRY M. MORRIS

Revised and Updated

MOODY PRESS

CHICAGO

Revised Edition

Original Title: *The Bible and Modern Science*

All Scripture quotations, unless noted otherwise, are from the King James Version.

Library of Congress Cataloging in Publication Data

Morris, Henry Madison, 1918-
  Science and the Bible.

  Bibliography: p.
  Includes index.
  1. Religion and science—1946-   I. Title.
BL240.2.M65   1986   220.1   86-16390
ISBN: 0-8024-0656-4 (pbk.)

9 10 11 12 Printing/LC/Year 94 93 92 91 90

Printed in the United States of America

Contents

Preface

"The purpose of this book, very frankly and without apology, is to win people to a genuine faith in Jesus Christ as the eternal Son of God and the Bible as the Word of God, and to help strengthen the faith of those who already believe. The Christian faith is not founded on wishful thinking or blind acceptance of tradition, but rather on a tremendous body of real, objective evidence."

The above paragraph introduced the 1951 edition of this book, as well as the 1956 and 1968 editions. (The book was first published in 1946 under the title *That You Might Believe*.) That stated purpose has been abundantly fulfilled, confirmed through the years by many wonderful letters and testimonies of conversions and spiritual growth. The purpose remains the same for this new edition.

A book on science and the Bible that has been kept continuously in print for over forty years can only be explained by the perennially vital importance of this subject, which seems to grow more significant every year. Never have there been more widespread and bitter attacks on biblical Christianity than there are today; but likewise never have the scientific evidences for the divine origin and truth of the Bible been so clear and strong. Consequently, it seems appropriate to prepare an updated edition of *Science and the Bible*.

Since so much has happened since the most recent edition was published in 1968, including the modern revival of creationism, this edition has been almost completely rewritten. It has also been slightly enlarged, but I trust it is still as easy to understand as before. The topics covered are the same; however I believe that the evidences for the truth of the Bible and the saving gospel of Jesus Christ are stronger and more convincing than ever.

As in previous editions, the text has been kept free of extensive footnotes in order to make it easier to read. However, for those readers who desire documentation as well as further information, an annotated bibliography is provided. The bibliography is not exhaustive, of course, but I believe it is representative. Most of the books listed are quite recent, and all are well worth reading.

The evidences discussed in *Science and the Bible* are mostly practical and objective rather than philosophical or experience-oriented. My own conviction, of course, is that every word of the Bible is true, inspired of God and absolutely free of error. Furthermore, there are today thousands of other scientists, not to mention multitudes of Christian believers in all walks of life who hold similar convictions. There is, indeed, good and sufficient evidence of the truth of God's Word for all who are willing to consider it.

The evidence can never be strong enough, however, to convince someone who is not *willing* to believe. If the evidence were so overwhelming as to *compel* one to believe it, there would be no room for faith, and God desires that we come to Him willingly, through His Son, in faith and love and gratitude. I can only urge the reader, therefore, to look at the evidence with an open mind and heart. It is my prayer that the Lord will use this new edition of *Science and the Bible* to lead many to a saving acceptance of Christ and to a life of strong faith and fruitful service in His name.

Acknowledgments

The manuscript for *Science and the Bible* has been reviewed for accuracy by the following specialists:

Malcolm A. Cutchins (Ph.D., professor of aerospace engineering, Auburn University)

Carl B. Fliermans (Ph.D., microbial ecologist, Dupont Company, Augusta, Georgia)

Donald D. Hamann (Ph.D., professor of food technology, North Carolina State University)

David Menton (Ph.D., associate professor of anatomy, Washington University, St. Louis)

John R. Meyer (Ph.D., professor of biology, Baptist Bible College, Clark's Summit, Pennsylvania)

John D. Morris (Ph.D., associate professor of geology, Institute for Creation Research)

John W. Oller (Ph.D., professor of linguistics, University of New Mexico)

John C. Whitcomb (Th.D., director of doctoral studies, Grace Theological Seminary)

I appreciate their many excellent suggestions, most of which have been incorporated in the book. I do, of course, take full responsibility for its final form.

I also thank my daughter, Mrs. Mary R. Smith, who typed the manuscript and has been of much help in getting it ready for publication. Ella K. Lindvall, managing editor at Moody Press, and her associates have also been most gracious and helpful in carrying it through to publication.

1

Science in the Bible

One of the most amazing evidences of the divine inspiration of the Bible is its scientific accuracy. There are many unexpected scientific truths that have lain hidden within its pages for thousands of years, only to be recognized and appreciated in recent times. These principles are not expressed in modern technical jargon, of course, but nevertheless are presented accurately and beautifully, indicating remarkable understanding of nature by these ancient authors far in advance of their "discovery" by modern scientists. Let us look at a few of these.

ASTRONOMY

Consider the field of astronomy, for example. Since ancient times, people have been fascinated by the stars, and many astronomers have tried to count them. Ptolemy counted 1,056. Tycho Brahe cataloged 777, and Johannes Kepler counted 1,005. The total number of stars visible to the naked eye is perhaps 4,000, counting all that are visible from every point on earth.

Yet the Bible had said that "the host of heaven cannot be

numbered" (Jeremiah 33:22), while also comparing "the sand which is upon the sea shore" to "the stars of the heaven" in multitude (Genesis 22:17). Before the invention of the telescope, this must have seemed like a serious scientific mistake in the Bible. Now, however, it must be recognized as a supernatural scientific insight. Astronomers estimate that there are at least 10^{26} stars (that is, a hundred-million-billion-billion stars), which reflects the same order of magnitude as the number of grains of sand on the earth. Truly, the stars cannot be numbered. If one could count 10 numbers per second, it would take him at least a thousand-million-billion years to count up to 10^{26}.

Look also at 1 Corinthians 15:41: "One star differeth from another star in glory." This must also have once seemed like a mistake, since every star (except the sun) looks just like a point of light, even through a telescope. Now, of course, it is known that there are many different types of stars, and no two stars are alike.

As far as our solar system is concerned, consider Psalm 19, which is often cited as an example of the Bible's "prescientific" perspective. In speaking of the sun, the psalmist says: "His going forth is from the end of the heaven, and his circuit unto the ends of it: and there is nothing hid from the heat thereof" (Psalm 19:6). It is claimed by critics that the writer of this verse must have believed in the unscientific notion that the sun revolves around the earth.

This claim is both unjust and unscientific itself, however. We still use words and phrases like "sunrise" and "sunset" simply because from our natural viewpoint, the sun does rise in the morning, move across the sky, and set in the evening. Navigators, surveyors, and astronomers commonly base their calculations on the assumption that the earth is the center of a great celestial sphere, along the surface of which, in ordered paths, move the sun, moon, planets, and stars. And as far as any practical usage is concerned, that is true. On this assumption, courses can be plotted, positions can be determined, and scores of other practical applications can be made.

As a matter of fact, however, the words of the psalmist may be even more scientific than he could have known. Studies of modern galactic astronomy have indicated that the sun is indeed moving around a center in the Milky Way galaxy in a gigantic orbit that would require two million centuries to complete, even at the tremendous tangential speed of 600,000 miles per hour. Furthermore, it is well known that our own galaxy is moving with respect to other galaxies. The sun's circuit *is* from one end of the heavens to the other.

In fact, no one knows where the center of the universe is. For all we *know* to the contrary, it could even be the earth. Every object is moving with respect to this unknown center, so that all motions must be measured in terms of "relative" motion, measured with respect to some *assumed* point of zero motion. This arbitrary reference point normally should be the point that makes the calculation easiest; and, in most cases, that would be on the earth's surface at the location of the observer. Consequently, the psalmist—instead of using prescientific language—was using the *most* scientific language he *could* have used in describing the motion of the sun relative to the earth.

It is wonderful to realize that the great Astronomer and Mathematician who created the heavens, setting all the stars and galaxies in their appointed courses and who "calleth them all by their names" (Psalm 147:4), is the same loving God who calls you and me to eternal life in Jesus Christ.

GEOPHYSICS

The science of geophysics ("physics of the earth") deals with the earth's shape, structure, and force systems. In this field also the biblical perspective is surprisingly modern.

It has been only a few centuries since the scientists and teachers all believed in a flat earth, and those intellectuals may well have thought the Bible was unscientific when it described a spherical earth. Isaiah, speaking of God, said: "It is he that sitteth upon the circle of the earth" (Isaiah 40:22). The word translated "circle" is the Hebrew *khug,* a more exact connotation of which is "sphericity" or "roundness." It is also used in Proverbs 8:27: "He set a compass upon the face of the depth [or 'deep']." The same word is here translated "compass," referring to the surface of the ocean taking on a spherical shape (the so-called "sea level") when God created it.

Today, of course, scientists all agree with the Bible in its teaching of a round earth. Sometimes critics claim that the Bible teaches a flat earth, but there is no such verse in the Bible.

Consider also Job 26:7: "[God] . . . hangeth the earth upon nothing." This is another example of twentieth-century science in the Bible. Even the existence of the hypothetical space substance called *ether* is rejected by most physicists and astronomers today. The force called gravity is invoked to account for the earth's affinity to the sun, but that doesn't *explain* anything, since no one knows what gravity is or why it works. How such a mysterious "action at a distance" could keep the earth attached to the sun, 93 million miles away, is quite unknown. There is no better explanation than that of Scripture: "He . . . hangeth the earth upon nothing."

HYDROLOGY

The field of hydrology ("science of water") is one with many biblical contacts, because of the major importance of water in the life of mankind. The most important and fundamental principle of this field is the water cycle—the remarkable mechanism by which water vapor is condensed and precipitated as rain or snow, then drained off through the groundwater and river system into the ocean, from which it is raised into the skies by evaporation and carried back over the continents by great atmospheric wind circulations.

The water cycle and its accompanying global atmospheric circulation have only been demonstrated scientifically in recent centuries, but they were set forth in the Bible ages ago. There are many relevant Bible references, all of which are fully in accord with scientific concepts, but one passage is especially comprehensive. This is Ecclesiastes 1:6–7, set down by Solomon three thousand years ago: "The wind goeth toward the south, and turneth about unto the north; it whirleth about continually, and the wind returneth again according to his circuits. All the rivers run into the sea; yet the sea is not full; unto the place from whence the rivers come, thither they return again." No wonder we speak of the wisdom of Solomon! This is a succinct yet comprehensive outline of the water cycle of the earth.

As an example of the many other references to one or another phase of the hydrologic cycle, look at the words of Elihu in Job 36:27–29: "For he draweth up the drops of water, which distil in rain from his vapor, which the skies pour down and drop upon man abundantly. Yea, can any understand the spreadings of the clouds, the thunderings of his pavilion?" (ASV*).

There is still much for man to learn concerning the details of the water cycle. Each phase of the cycle is absolutely necessary for life to exist on the earth and offers abundant testimony to its origin at the hands of an infinitely wise and beneficent Creator. With so many references in the Bible to water in all its aspects, it is significant that there are none that conflict with modern hydrologic science.

BIOLOGY

The great truth revealed in Leviticus 17:11 and a number of other Scripture verses concerning the preeminent importance of blood in the biological mechanism was written thousands of years in advance of the discovery of the circulation of the blood

* *American Standard Version.*

by William Harvey in 1616: "For the life of the flesh is in the blood."

Continuance of life is now known to depend upon the continued supply of oxygen, water, and food to the cells of the body. This essential function is accomplished in a marvelous manner by the blood as it circulates constantly throughout the body, year after year. The role of blood in combating disease-producing organisms and in repairing injured tissues is one of the most significant discoveries of medical science, and the use of blood transfusions as one of the most beneficial treatments for many medical needs further testifies to the supreme importance of the blood in the life of the flesh.

The Word of God was scientifically accurate in this great biological truth long before scientists discovered and elaborated it. Yet it was given primarily to teach an even greater spiritual truth—the necessity of the shedding of blood in sacrifice for the remission of sins. The blood, which is the channel of life, becomes also the carrier of disease and infection through the body when they gain the upper hand in the system. Physical life and death symbolize spiritual life and death, just as physical disease and injury symbolize the spiritual disease of sin.

As the infection of sin spreads throughout the soul, it will eventually, "when it is finished, bringeth forth death" (James 1:15), and this is spiritual death, eternal separation from God in hell. If spiritual life is to be created and maintained, it must come from outside. It must be life untainted with sin and containing the power to combat the sin-disease in the spiritually dying soul. Figuratively speaking, a blood transfusion is essential from a qualified donor whose blood possesses the purity and efficacy required for the cleansing and healing of the mortally sin-sick soul.

This is just a glimpse of the tremendous spiritual (and even biological) meaning in the biblical doctrine of substitutionary sacrifice. "Without shedding of blood is no remission" (Hebrews 9:22). This was the symbolism of the animal sacrifices in the Mosaic law. Its ultimate fulfillment was in the sacrificial death of the Son of God for the sins of the world. Jesus said, "This is my blood of the new testament, which is shed for many for the remission of sins" (Matthew 26:28).

By virtue of the substitutionary death of the Lord Jesus Christ, each one who receives by faith His life—poured out unto death but raised up again by the power of God—receives forgiveness and cleansing of all sin and, in fact, receives Christ Himself. All this is portrayed by the shed blood of Christ. Christ said, "Whoso eateth my flesh, and drinketh my blood, hath eternal life; and I will raise him up at the last day. . . . He that eateth my flesh, and drinketh my blood, dwelleth in me, and I in him" (John 6:54, 56).

THE BASIC LAWS OF SCIENCE

Even more significant than the many specific facts of science in the Bible is the remarkable truth that the most universal principles of science are also there. These are the laws of energy conservation and deterioration. The law of energy conservation states that in a closed system, in any transformation of energy from one form of energy into another (and everything that happens involves such energy transformations), the total amount of energy in the system remains unchanged. No energy is either created or destroyed. A similar law is the law of mass conservation, which states that although matter may be changed in state, density, or form, its total mass is unchanged. In other words, these basic laws teach that no creation or destruction of matter or energy is now being accomplished anywhere in the physical universe. Since matter and energy are themselves interchangeable under certain conditions, the two laws can be combined into the principle that the total of mass-plus-energy is conserved.

These conservation laws were not demonstrated quantitatively by scientists until the nineteenth century. However, the

Bible has taught for thousands of years the same great truth—
that genuine creation is no longer taking place, contrary to the
evolutionary philosophy of continuing creation. For example,
Hebrews 4:3 says, "The works were finished from the foundation of the world." The account of creation concludes with the
summary statement: "Thus the heavens and the earth were
finished, and all the host of them. And on the seventh day God
ended his work which he had made" (Genesis 2:1–2).

This law of mass-and-energy conservation, also known as
the first law of thermodynamics, is generally recognized as the
most important and basic law of science.

The second law of thermodynamics, almost as great in
significance as the first, states the corollary principle of mass/
energy deterioration. In any energy conversion, although the
total amount of energy remains unchanged (Hebrews 1:3 says
that Christ is "upholding all things by the word of his power"),
the amount of usefulness and availability that the energy possesses is always decreased. This principle is also called the law
of entropy increase; entropy being a sort of mathematical ab-
straction that is actually a measure of the nonavailability of the
energy of a system.

Thus, in any isolated system (that is, a system from which
all external sources of energy are shut off), the energy of the
system is conserved in quantity but is continually being de-
graded in quality as long as any energy change is taking place in
the system. Some of the available energy is always dissipated in
nonrecoverable friction or heat energy. Since all activities of
nature (including biological activities) involve such energy trans-
fers, there must be an ever-decreasing supply of usable energy
for maintaining all natural processes in the universe as a whole.

This law of entropy increase is responsible for the fact that
no machine can be constructed to 100 percent efficiency and for
the fact that a perpetual motion machine is impossible. Practically all the earth's energy comes, or has come, from the sun,
but most of the tremendous energy output of the sun is dissi-

pated in space in the form of unrecoverable heat energy. This prodigious waste of energy cannot last forever. Eventually, barring supernatural intervention, the sun must burn itself out, and then all activity on the earth must cease as well. The same principle applies to all the stars of the universe, so that the physical universe is, beyond any question, growing old, wearing out, and running down.

But this in turn means that the universe had a definite beginning. If it is growing old, it must once have been young; if it is wearing out, it must first have been new; if it is running down, it must originally have been "wound up." In short, this law of energy degeneration conveys us inexorably back to the necessary truth of the existence of a Creator and a definite creation, which must have been taken place in the past but which, according to the conservation principle, is *not* continuing in the present.

Scripture frequently refers to this principle of universal deterioration. For example, "Of old hast thou laid the foundation of the earth: and the heavens are the work of thy hands. They shall perish, but thou shalt endure: yea, all of them shall wax old like a garment; as a vesture shalt thou change them, and they shall be changed: But thou art the same, and thy years shall have no end" (Psalm 102:25–27).

There are many other similar passages in the Bible (e.g., Romans 8:20–22). Thus, the Scriptures teach what science has only discovered in the past hundred years or so—namely, that in spite of an original completed creation, the universe is aging and heading inexorably toward ultimate physical death.

However, the Bible also reveals something that science could never predict: a future supernatural intervention of the Creator in His creation, destruction of the present system, and creation of a "new heaven and a new earth," which "shall remain" and "wherein dwelleth righteousness" (Revelation 21:1; Isaiah 65:17; 66:22; 2 Peter 3:13).

MATTER AND ENERGY

An allied truth is also indicated in Scripture. That is the essential equivalence of matter and energy—one of the most important discoveries of twentieth-century science. According to the famous equation of Albert Einstein, energy is equal to matter multiplied by the square of the velocity of light. Thus, matter is essentially a manifestation of that form of energy known as atomic energy. The ultimate source of the tremendous energy locked in the atom is unknown and perhaps undiscoverable by science. The magnitude of this energy or power (where power is the *rate* of energy per unit of time), which maintains the terrific motions and forces associated with the various subatomic particles, is evident in the fantastic power released in atomic disintegrations. Thus, the ultimate nature of matter is power.

This basic principle of our nuclear age was suggested long ago in the proclamation of Hebrews 1:1-3, "God . . . hath in these last days spoken unto us by his Son, whom he hath appointed heir of all things, by whom also he made the worlds; who being the brightness of his glory, and the express image of his person, and upholding all things by the word of his power, when he had by himself purged our sins, sat down on the right hand of the Majesty on high."

That is, *things* are upheld by *power*. And the source of that power is the Creator Himself, the Lord Jesus Christ. This same tremendous truth is taught in Colossians 1:17, "By him [Christ] all things consist." The verb here is the Greek word from which we transliterate our English word *sustain* and could well be translated "hold together."

In Hebrews 11:3 we find the following remarkable statement: "Through faith we understand that the worlds were framed by the word of God, so that things which are seen were not made of things which do appear." The matter of the universe is not ultimately physical but is composed of something that is not apparent. It was all "framed," or formed, by the omnipotent word, not out of primeval matter in some chaotic form, but *ex nihilo*, "out of nothing," except the power of God.

The Greek word for "worlds" in this verse is essentially *aeons*. It means "world-times," or better, "space-times." In this context, it anticipates the scientific concept of the cosmos as a *continuum* of space and time and matter.

Thus, not only is the material substance of the universe upheld by the divine Word; it was also called into existence by that same divine Word. It is significant that the marvelous faith chapter found in Hebrews 11 begins with such an eloquent assertion of the necessity of understanding—by faith—the fact of a primeval special creation. The foundation of all faith must be faith in genuine *ex nihilo* creation and in God (Christ) as personal Creator.

THE TRI-UNIVERSE

An amazing revelation of modern science is the fact that the physical universe is a *tri-universe*—a trinity of trinities—perfectly modeling the nature of the Triune God who made it. All true Christians believe in the doctrine of the Trinity: God is one God manifest in three divine Persons—Father, Son, and Holy Spirit. We do *not* believe in three gods (that would be polytheism) but *one* God. Yet each of the three distinct Persons is fully and eternally that one God.

How can that be? It seems impossible, and many people scoff at Christians' trinitarian beliefs. It is contrary to sound mathematics, they say, for Christians to maintain that $1 + 1 + 1 = 1$ rather than 3. Since such a system is unscientific, they say, then neither the Son nor the Spirit can really be God.

However, the fact is that the universe itself manifests exactly the same type of triune character that the Bible attributes to God. In a very real way, "the invisible things of him from the creation of the world are clearly seen, being understood by the things that are made, even his eternal power and Godhead'' (Romans 1:20). That is, His "Godhead" is understood by "the things that are made," having been "clearly seen" from the creation of the world.

The doctrine of the Trinity is nowhere set forth in the Bible as an explicit doctrine. It appears indirectly yet perfectly naturally as the Lord Jesus speaks of Himself, the Father, and the Holy Spirit. The logical order presented is: (1) God the Father—the unseen source and cause of all things, (2) God the Son—who tangibly reveals the Father to man and who executes the will of God, and (3) God the Holy Spirit—who is (like the Father) unseen and yet reveals the Son to men, especially through the holy Scriptures that He inspired, making real in the hearts and lives of men the experience of fellowship with the Son and the Father. This order, however, is not an order of importance or length of existence. All are equally eternal and equally God—one God. The Son is eternally the only begotten of the Father; the Spirit is eternally proceeding from the Father through the Son.

The remarkable fact is that these relationships are beautifully patterned in the physical universe. Everything in this universe can be understood as functioning as a continuum of space, matter, and time. Space is the invisible, omnipresent background of all things, manifesting itself always and everywhere in phenomena of matter and/or energy, which are then interpreted and experienced through time. These are analogous to the relationships in the Godhead between Father, Son, and Spirit; the one is a perfect model of the other.

Note that the universe is a tri-universe. It is not part space, part time, and part matter (that would be a triad) but *all* space, *all* time and *all* matter (where matter includes energy, with matter/energy permeating all space and time). This is a true trinity.

Furthermore, each component of this tri-universe is also a trinity. Space consists of three dimensions, each of which is equally important and occupies all space. There could be no space—no reality—if there were only two dimensions. All dimensions are necessary, yet there is just one space, and each dimension comprises the whole of space. Note that to calculate the amount of a given space, one does not *add* its three dimensions but *multiplies* them. Analogously, the mathematics of the divine Trinity is not $1 + 1 + 1 = 1$ but rather $1 \times 1 \times 1 = 1$. Space is always identified in terms of one dimension but is only seen in two dimensions and experienced in three dimensions.

Similarly, time is one entity but can also be conceptualized as future, present, and past time. Each involves the whole of time, yet each is distinct—though each is meaningless without the other two. The future is the unseen, unexperienced source of time; the present is time being "seen," or manifested; the past is time experienced but no longer seen. The unseen future becomes manifest in the present; the past proceeds from the future through the present into the realm of past experience. Again, the same interrelationships apply as for the Persons of the Godhead.

The central entity in the tri-universe is *matter,* which is essentially unseen energy manifesting itself in motion and experienced in various phenomena. These phenomena all occur in space through time. Unseen but omnipresent energy generates motion, the magnitude of which (velocity) is the ratio of the space to the time. Depending on the rates and types of motion, various phenomena (e.g., light, sound, texture, hardness) are experienced. For example, light energy generates light waves that are experienced in seeing light. It is always thus: unseen energy generating motion that is experienced in phenomena—this is matter, and each of its three components again comprises the whole.

Thus the physical universe is actually a trinity of trinities, a true tri-universe in the fullest sense. But this same remarkable phenomenon can be seen in the realm of human life as well.

The Bible says that men and women were created in God's image.

Note that each individual is a person with a body that can be physically heard, seen, and touched. But inside that body is the person's nature, which is unseen and yet is the source of all that he embodies. On the other hand, the person is known to others only through his personality, which is unseen and intangible, yet is the means by which he and his nature exert influence on others. Human life thus consists of three entities— nature, person, and personality—each of which pervades the whole of his life and yet is distinct from the other two. The nature is the unseen source, revealed and embodied in the person. The personality proceeds from the person, invisible yet influencing the lives of others in regard to the person. Nature, person, and personality (or, perhaps equivalently, soul, body, and spirit) thus constitute a true trinity, reflecting in minute detail the Triuneness of the God who created the human trinity.

This same three-in-one character seems to pervade everything in life. Every moral action consists of (1) the motive, (2) the act, and (3) the consequence and meaning. Similarly, all forms of thought or reason proceed logically from the universal to the particular to the relationship of the particular thing to other things. Everything that happens proceeds from the cause to the event to its effects—from the source to its manifestation to its meaning. Always the same types of interrelatedness and of triune wholeness in three exist everywhere.[1]

Although these remarkable facts cannot be held to *prove* that the Creator of the universe and life is a Triune Being, it is difficult to conceive of any other cause that could account for such effects. If the universe is intelligible and the principle of cause and effect (no effect greater than its cause) really is valid

1. Many of these trinitarian relationships were first pointed out by Nathan Wood in his book *The Secret of the Universe* (1936), later reprinted under the title *The Trinity in the Universe* (Grand Rapids: Kregel, 1978).

(and all science is based on this assumption), then there is certainly overwhelming reason to believe in the Triune God of the Bible. The doctrine of the Trinity is not a logical absurdity, as some would claim, but a scientific living reality. God was manifested and revealed by and in His Son, who as a man was Jesus Christ. There can, therefore, be nothing in life more important for any individual than to become rightly related to this tri-universe and its Triune God. This means unreserved acceptance of the Lord Jesus Christ, for "in him dwelleth all the fulness of the Godhead bodily" (Colossians 2:9).

THE QUESTION OF MIRACLES

Most of the scientific "errors" that critics claim to have found in the Bible involve its alleged miracles. The virgin birth of Christ, for example, is rejected because it is said to be unscientific. His resurrection must have been a spiritual resurrection, because a bodily resurrection from the dead is scientifically impossible. In fact, it is claimed that real miracles never happen because they are scientifically impossible, so any report of a miracle must be mistaken or false according to naturalistic scientists and other skeptics.

But all such claims are beside the point. Miracles, indeed, are scientifically impossible—in fact, that is the very definition of a miracle. The question is not whether a miracle is possible but whether it happens. To deny that miracles are possible is to deny that God exists.

It is a question of evidence. Miracles are certainly possible, though they are bound to be rare since God's created laws of nature are good laws, and He is not capricious. He will only intervene in His established laws if there is good reason to do so, in accordance with His great purposes in creation and redemption. In the case of the biblical miracles, there is always good reason for every miracle reported, as well as good evidence that they all really happened.

Since a miracle is, by definition, an event that sets aside or modifies one or more laws or processes of nature, it is helpful to remember that the two basic laws of science (i.e., known laws of nature) are the first and second laws of thermodynamics—the law of conservation and the law of deterioration discussed previously. The first says that in any isolated, natural system, the matter/energy of the system is neither created nor destroyed. The second says that the entropy (or disorganization) of the system must increase.

Therefore, any event in which the energy or matter or organization is suddenly increased in a isolated system would require an act of special creation and would be a miracle. Both the virgin birth and the resurrection are examples, as are Christ's multiplication of the loaves and fish, the handwriting on Belshazzar's wall, and many other biblical miracles. These are miracles of creation, or "Grade-A" miracles.

There is a second type of miracle—one that does not require the intervention of special creation in a natural process—but which does involve an unusual statistical deviation from the normal rate and circumstance at which the process functions. Every natural process is affected by many factors; a change in any one will change its rate or location or time of occurrence. Thus, every process operates statistically around an average—sometimes more, sometimes less. If a particular occurrence involves an unusual rate or time, it could be recognized as a miracle of providence, or a "Grade-B" miracle. An example would be the feeding of Elijah by the ravens; another would be the abnormal catch of fish by the disciples when the Lord told them to cast their nets.

If my count is reasonably correct, the Bible describes about 89 Grade-A miracles and about 127 Grade-B miracles.[2] The

2. Henry M. Morris, *The Biblical Basis for Modern Science* (Grand Rapids: Baker, 1984), pp. 75–101, 466–74. About sixteen satanic or demonic miracles are described in the Bible.

latter often involve the special agency of angels, who evidently have the knowledge and power to control the rate and timing of natural processes to some degree.

In any case, there is no scientific justification for anyone to doubt any of the miracles of the Bible. Each miracle can be defended both on the basis of need and actual evidence of the miracle. For example, let us consider two of the miracles that have been objects of the greatest skepticism.

JONAH'S WHALE

The record of Jonah and the whale has been difficult for many to believe. Some have claimed that no whale possesses a gullet large enough to admit a man. However, it is now known that the sperm whale, which inhabits the Mediterranean, is quite capable of swallowing an object much larger than a man, and the same is true of the whale shark and other great marine animals. Both the Hebrew and Greek words used in reference to Jonah's "whale" could actually apply to any great marine monster.

As a matter of fact, there have been in modern times a number of evidently well-verified instances of whales and sharks swallowing men alive and even one or two cases of men's actually surviving such an experience. Even if they are true, however, these cases are beside the point, since the Bible clearly sets forth Jonah's experience as a miracle. The great fish was both prepared by God and controlled by God throughout (Jonah 1:17; 2:10). The miracle may even have involved restoring Jonah to life after he had died (Jonah 2:6) and his soul gone to "hell" (Heb., *sheol*; Jonah 2:2), which is the place of departed spirits.

The question simply is, Is the story of Jonah history or merely an allegory (as liberals allege)? The account itself is presented as authentic history, detailing the conversion of multitudes of inhabitants of a real city—the great Assyrian city of

Nineveh (Jonah 3:5). Jonah is mentioned as a real prophet in 2 Kings 14:25, and the entire record of Jonah was accepted as historical by all ancient Jewish historians and commentators. It is hard to believe these could all have been mistaken, having been much closer geographically and chronologically to the events than the modern liberals are.

The compelling reason for accepting the record of Jonah as historical, of course, is because it was so accepted by the Lord Jesus Christ Himself. "The men of Nineveh," He said, "repented at the preaching of Jonas" (Luke 11:32). With respect to the miracle of the great fish, He said: "For as Jonas was three days and three nights in the whale's belly; so shall the Son of man be three days and three nights in the heart of the earth" (Matthew 12:40). Thus He appropriated Jonah's miraculous preservation and restoration as a type and prophecy of His own soon-coming death, burial, and bodily resurrection. It is far easier to believe in the story of Jonah and the whale than it is to believe that the Lord was either lying or mistaken. The evidences for His own resurrection, which will be discussed later in this book, are irrefutable, and there can be no legitimate doubt of the fact that He both knows the truth and tells the truth.

THE LONG DAY

Perhaps the most tremendous miracle recorded in the Bible, except for the resurrection of Christ and the original creation itself, is the long day of Joshua, described in Joshua 10:11–14. This incredible story tells that, in the battle between the Israelites and the Amorite confederation, "the Lord fought for Israel" (v. 14) by two related miracles: (1) causing the sun to stand still in the midst of heaven, so that it "hasted not to go down about a whole day" (v. 13) in order to give the children of Israel time to defeat the Amorites completely before they could escape and regroup under cover of darkness; and (2) sending a devastating hailstorm, which probably served the twofold purpose of giving Joshua's army relief from the heat and of slaying large numbers of the enemy (Joshua 10:11).

Since the sun and moon both "stood still" for an extra day (note the discussion of relative motion on pp. 12-13), it seems clear that the earth stopped rotating on its axis, and the moon also stopped its motion about the earth. This might even mean that the entire solar system stopped its various motions for a day.

In any case, it was a mighty miracle, and even many Christians have been reluctant to accept it at face value. Some have suggested that there was a sort of prolonged "looming mirage" effect, or a lengthened and intensified atmospheric refraction of some kind that made the sun just *seem* to stay in the midst of the sky for a day. Others have said that God gave the Israelite army supernatural strength that enabled them to accomplish in one day what ordinarily would have required two days.

Such explanations would still require a Grade-A miracle of *some* kind, and they would have to be at the expense of accusing Joshua (and the Holy Spirit) of confusing the account of the miracle by using misleading language to describe it. It is far better to take God's words at face value. He is able to say what He means. A miracle is a miracle, and one is no more difficult than another for the Creator.

The question is not, Could it occur? but, Did it occur? What is the historical evidence? A related question would have to do with God's reason for causing such a tremendous interruption in His created laws for the solar system. Further, what was the significance of the accompanying hailstorm?

Another frequent objection is that if the earth suddenly stopped rotating on its axis, everything on the surface would be violently dislocated and probably destroyed. But why infer restrictions on God's ability to accomplish the miracle in whatever way would best fulfill His purpose? The Bible does not suggest that the stoppage was sudden. If an automobile traveling at high speed is instantaneously stopped, great damage ensues to its occupants; but if it gradually slows down to a halt, they feel no disturbance.

It is true, of course, that when the earth was slowing down, the circulation of the atmosphere would be drastically affected, since it is controlled to a great extent by the earth's rotation. That fact may well account for the tremendous hailstorm that accompanied the miracle.

Furthermore, even though the account in Joshua doesn't mention it specifically, there are evidences that the land surfaces may indeed have been profoundly disturbed at this time. A vision of the prophet Habakkuk reflects back on the time that "the sun and moon stood still in their habitation," and in the context, Habakkuk also refers to such phenomena as: "the everlasting mountains were scattered"; "thou didst cleave the earth with rivers"; "the deep uttered his voice"; and others (Habakkuk 3:11, 6, 9, 10). The "hailstones" accompanying the long day may not have been the same as the "great stones from heaven" (Joshua 10:11) that also fell, since the word for "stones" in this case is normally used specifically for rocks.

In any case, the main question is whether a long day ever occurred in world history. Such an event was also recorded in an ancient book called "the book of Jasher" (Joshua 10:13). Apart from the biblical record, of course, such an event would now have to be preserved mainly in the form of semimythical recollections handed down in the folklore of various tribes and nations. Written records from that period (about 1400 B.C.) are scarce and fragmentary.

However, it is significant that suggestions of a long day (or long night, in the Western Hemisphere) are, indeed, noted in the mythologies of many peoples from various parts of the earth. So frequently do these occur, in fact, that atheists have even used that fact to argue that the Joshua account was based on such traditions. For example, T. W. Doane, in his book *Bible Myths* (New York: Truth Seeker, 1882, p. 91), describes accounts of a long day or long night in the Orphic hymns and in the legends of the Hindus, the Buddhists, the Chinese, the ancient Mexicans, and others, and then strangely argues that that fact proves the biblical record to be merely a myth.

In a 1945 report to the Smithsonian Institution, M. W. Stirling notes that many American Indian tribes have a legend about the theft of the sun for a day. A similar legend is found among the Polynesians. The Greek legend of Phaeton, who disrupted the sun's course for a day, could easily have been derived from this event. The Greek historian Herodotus states that the priests of Egypt showed him records of such a day.

The widely publicized ideas of Immanuel Velikovsky should also be noted here. In this book *Worlds in Collision* (first published by Macmillan in 1950 and later by Doubleday, when a threatened boycott by the scientific establishment forced Macmillan to withdraw it), Dr. Velikovsky argued strongly for the historicity of Joshua's long day, supporting his case by an impressive list of testimonies from legends, inscriptions, and other ancient records from many places. He did not try to defend the Bible, since he himself was an atheist, but rather tried to explain the long day as having been caused by the gravitational and electromagnetic forces caused by a near-miss collision of the planet Venus with the earth at the time of Joshua. Other subsequent writers have tried to defend and extend similar ideas, including some Christian writers (e.g., Donald Patten, Ronald Hatch, and Loren Steinhauer in their book *The Long Day of Joshua and Six Other Catastrophes,* published by Baker in 1973).

Most scientists including myself feel that such an astral catastrophe is highly questionable and involves numerous difficulties if developed on a naturalistic premise. On the other hand, if God were going to use His miraculous power to produce the long day, it would certainly not be necessary to invoke Venus or some other astral body to do it for Him.

In any case, the question before us is simply: Did such an amazing event as the long day really happen? The answer, based on the statistical abundance of historical evidence, even ignoring the divinely inspired account in Scripture, has to be affirmative.

There have been some Christian writers who have argued that astronomical records have actually turned up a missing day in ancient history. Charles Totten in the nineteenth century maintained that this could be shown by counting backward from the present and forward from the date of creation (the latter being based on a chronology developed among the so-called British-Israelites, of which he was a leader), with their intersections showing a missing day of the week. In recent decades, some writers have alleged that the same result had been obtained by a NASA computer study (the latter, however, has never been documented and has been denied by NASA officials). Any such calculation would obviously have to be based on a known beginning point sometime earlier in history than the long day and, therefore, would involve one or more completely arbitrary assumptions. It is, therefore, quite unwise (as well as unnecessary) for Christians to cite this particular type of study as proof of the long day.

As far as God's reasons for such a miracle are concerned, the strategic importance of complete victory over the Amorites in Israel's conquest of Canaan is the basic reason. The success of Joshua's entire campaign depended on victory in this battle, and thus, also, the fulfillment of God's promises to the world through the nation of Israel. A second reason may well have been the fact that the Canaanites, the Egyptians, and other ancient peoples were all evolutionary pantheists who placed special emphasis on worshiping the sun as the source of all life and power on earth. It may have been that God chose to control the sun in such a way as to show all these nations that He, not the sun, was supreme. In that way, He both demonstrated the futility of their cruel and immoral religious systems and the fact that He had commissioned the Israelites, who worshiped the true God of creation, to remove that false religion from His specially chosen land of witness.

CONCLUSION

There are many other miracles in the Bible, which space in a small book will not permit us to discuss. A careful analysis of each, however, would show that each is supported by both adequate theological justification and also by adequate historical evidence.

Furthermore, there are many more points of scientific contact with the Bible than we have been able to discuss here.[3] In every case, the Bible can be shown to be scientifically accurate, often far in advance of its time.

There are, of course, two significant points of serious conflict between the biblical record and the standard position of the scientific establishment. These are the accounts in Genesis of the six-day period of special creation and the Noahic worldwide Flood, both of which are explicitly repudiated by most modern scientists and intellectuals. The truth is, however, that the facts of science support the Bible in these cases also, as will be shown in the next two chapters.

3. For an extensive discussion of all relevant fields of science in their relations to the Bible, please see my book *The Biblical Basis for Modern Science* (Grand Rapids: Baker, 1984).

2

The Theory of Evolution

The creation-evolution question is certainly the most important area of apparent conflict between the Bible and science. It is a great mistake for Christians to compromise on this issue or, perhaps even worse, to ignore it. Although our nation was founded on creationist principles and all the early schools in our country taught creation, evolution has now become the dominant philosophy and for several generations has been taught as fact in practically all our schools, from elementary schools to university graduate schools. Evolutionary assumptions also dominate the news media and all our public institutions. It has probably contributed more to the prevalent secularistic and materialistic philosophy of the world today than any other influence. It seems obvious that an issue that is so vitally significant ought to be seriously studied by all thinking men and women.

EVOLUTION VERSUS THE BIBLE

Evolution is not really a science at all; it is a philosophy or an attitude of mind. Evolutionists admit that no one has ever seen any real evolution (from one kind of creature to a more complex kind of creature) take place. Many animals have become extinct within the few thousand years of written records that we have, but no new kinds of animals have evolved during that period. Although evolutionists believe these great evolutionary changes must have taken place over the hundreds of millions of years of supposed earth history, none of these speculations can be proved or even tested. No man was present to observe and record them, so such ideas are entirely outside the scope of real science. Evolution must be *believed,* not observed. It is a matter of faith, not science.

The Bible, of course, teaches that the work of creation was all accomplished and completed in the six days of the creation week, as outlined in Genesis 1, whereas evolutionists contend that the *process* of "creation" (meaning evolution) has been going on for billions of years in the past and is still going on in the present. Scripture could hardly be more definite on this point: "Thus the heavens and the earth were finished, and all the host of them. . . . And God blessed the seventh day, and sanctified it: because that in it he had rested from all his work which God created and made" (Genesis 2:1, 3). Similarly in the New Testament, whenever God's work of creating the universe and all its creatures is mentioned, it is always in the past tense (e.g., Colossians 1:16: "For by him were all things created."). Note also Hebrews 4:3: "[God's] works were finished from the foundation of the world." This biblical revelation is, of course, in accord with the basic laws of science as discussed in the preceding chapter. By the conservation principle, nothing is now being created, just as Genesis says. By the entropy principle, there must have been a creation in the past, just as Genesis says. There is no such process going on today, just as Genesis says.

Although this is the most basic point of conflict between evolution and the Bible, there are numerous others. Most evolutionary biochemists think that living organisms first evolved out of nonliving chemicals in the primeval "soup" perhaps 3 billion

years ago, although there is another school of thought that
believes life evolved from clay minerals in the primeval lands.
Then, perhaps a billion years ago, multicelled invertebrate marine animals somehow evolved from one-celled organisms in the
ocean. Eventually marine vertebrates (fish) developed, then amphibians, reptiles, mammals, and birds, in order. Finally, perhaps 2 million years ago, man (at the stage of the genus *Homo*)
evolved from some as-yet-uncertain "hominid" ancestor. This
account is essentially the current evolutionary scenario advocated by most evolutionary biologists and paleontologists
today.

But that order of events does not correspond at all to the
order in Genesis. The latter indicates that all land plants, including even fruit trees, were made on the third day, whereas
marine organisms were not created until the fifth day of creation
week. (Evolutionists say that land plants, especially fruit trees,
evolved long after fish and other marine animals.) The Bible also
states that the birds were made at the same time as the fish.
According to Scripture, the "creeping things" (a term that
includes insects according to Leviticus 11:20–23) were among
the last things created (Genesis 1:25) just before man; but
insects evolved very early according to evolutionary paleontologists.

The sun and moon, according to Genesis, were not made
until the fourth day, halfway through the creation period. Not
only is that contrary to evolutionary geology, but such an order
would be completely lethal to the vegetation created on the third
day, if the days were longer than twenty-four hours. There are
many other contradictions between the order of creation in
Genesis and the order of evolution in historical geology.

The so-called "day-age theory" attempts to equate the
geological ages with the creation week of Genesis, but there are
too many flagrant contradictions between the two for any such
device to be acceptable to one who has not already placed an
unyielding faith in these geological ages. Although the Hebrew

word for "day" (*yom*) can occasionally mean a time of indefinite length if the context requires, such usage is rare, and the word almost always *does* mean a literal day (i.e., either a twenty-four-hour period or the daylight portion of that period). In Genesis, the context actually *precludes* any sort of indefinite meaning. The use of a numeral with *day* ("first day," and so on) or the use of boundary terms ("evening and morning") are usages that elsewhere in the Pentateuch invariably require the literal meaning of "day."

Conclusive proof that the "days" of Genesis are to be understood as literal days is found in the Ten Commandments. The fourth commandment says: "Remember the Sabbath day, to keep it holy. Six days shalt thou labour, and do all thy work: but the seventh day is the sabbath of the Lord thy God: in it thou shalt not do any work. . . . For in six days the Lord made heaven and earth, the sea, and all that in them is, and rested the seventh day" (Exodus 20:8–11).

It is clear from the strong wording that God used in this commandment (written with His own finger on a table of stone, according to Exodus 31:18) that the "days" of God's week are exactly equivalent to the days of man's week. Furthermore, the word twice translated "days" in this passage (Heb., *yamim*) occurs more than seven hundred times elsewhere in the Old Testament and always means literal days. It is well to note also that there is at least one good word (Heb., *olam*) that means "age" or "long, indefinite time," and this word should have been used in Genesis 1 and Exodus 20 if that were the writer's intended meaning. The fact that He used the words "day" and "days" without any hint in the context of a nonliteral meaning, makes it evident that He intended the literal meaning. If the creation days *were* literal days, of course, then evolution would be completely out of the question.

There is still another important biblical emphasis that completely precludes any real evolution. The phrase "after its kind(s)" is used no less than ten times in the first chapter of Genesis.

Every created "kind" (Heb., *min*) was to reproduce after its own kind and not to generate some new kind. This does not preclude "horizontal" variation within limits (e.g., the different varieties of dogs or cats or people), but it does prohibit "vertical" variation from one kind to some higher kind (e.g., monkeys to men). This truth is also stressed again in the New Testament (e.g., 1 Corinthians 15:38–39).

A person therefore is compelled to make a choice, either to believe the Bible or to believe in evolution. It is impossible really to believe in both, because each fully contradicts the other.

THEISM VERSUS EVOLUTION

There are, of course, many people who do not believe in biblical inerrancy (and who, therefore, would not be swayed by anti-evolutionary statements in the Bible) but who do believe in God and who believe that God somehow used evolution as His method of creation.

However, regardless of what the Bible says, those who seek to honor God should realize that evolution is naturalistic and materialistic by its very nature. It is merely an attempt to explain the origin of things without God. Naturalism and chance constitute the very essence of evolution.

Evolution is also in conflict with the teachings of Christ. He should not have healed the lame and the sick if progress is measured by the "survival of the fittest." He taught self-sacrifice, but evolution is necessarily based on self-preservation in the struggle for existence.

Evolution is also the most inefficient and cruel method for creating man that could be conceived. If God is a God of love and wisdom and power (as the Bible teaches), then how could He ever be guilty of devising such a scheme as evolution? What possible reason could there have been for such flesh-eating monsters as Tyrannosaurus Rex, for example, to rule the earth for 100 million years, only to die out about seventy million years before man evolved? If the geological ages really took place and if man was not merely the end but in fact the goal of the evolutionary process as "theistic evolutionists" believe, then multiplied billions of animals have suffered and died for no apparent reason. The account of creation in Genesis ends with the conclusion that everything God had made was, in His judgment, "very good" (Genesis 1:31). Surely God could not possibly have viewed the fossilized remains of billions upon billions of His creatures in the rocks of the earth's crust as "very good" if such fossils really marked the end of His "creation" period. The Bible says that death only entered the world as a result of man's sin (Romans 5:12; 1 Corinthians 15:21) and will be removed once sin is removed (Revelation 21:4, 27), but evolution requires suffering and death as an integral part of the very process that brought man into the world. Thus theistic evolution is a contradiction in terms. If one wishes to believe in evolution, he is free to make that choice, but he certainly should not associate a wise, powerful, loving God with such a monstrous system.

Furthermore, the antitheistic character of the doctrine of evolution is evidenced in the multitude of anti-Christian social philosophies and anti-moral social practices the system has spawned. On one hand, evolution has been claimed as the scientific rationale for socialism, communism, anarchism, and many other "left-wing" movements. On the other hand, philosophers of the so-called "right-wing" have taken the Darwinian concepts of "struggle" and "survival of the fittest" and used them to justify many harmful systems such as Nazism, racism, imperialism, and laissez-faire capitalism. Marx, Lenin, and Stalin were ardent evolutionists but so were Haeckel, Nietzsche, and Hitler. The first two tenets of secular humanism (as expressed in the famous 1933 Humanist Manifesto) dealt with the assumed evolution of the universe and mankind. Any form of atheism or pantheism or occultism must necessarily be based on evolution. Determinism, existentialism, behaviorism, Freudianism, and other such amoral psychological systems are grounded in evolutionary theory.

Modern evolutionary scientists often vigorously protest when these facts are called to the attention of lay audiences. Nevertheless, they *are facts,* as can easily be documented from the writings of the founders and leaders of each of the above systems.

Furthermore, evolutionism is profoundly philosophical and religious—*not* scientific. It is amazing that educators can decry creationism and get it banned from public institutions on the grounds of separation of church and state when evolutionism itself has, in effect, become institutionalized as *the* one and only state religion, both in capitalistic and noncapitalistic societies.

Evolution, in fact, is not only the basic premise of all atheistic and humanistic religions but also of the various pantheistic religions, occult religions, and animistic religions. The great ethnic religions—Taoism, Buddhism, Confucianism, Hinduism, and other such faiths—are all essentially based on some form of evolution, accepting the space-time cosmos as the only ultimate and eternal reality and denying any real transcendent Creator of the cosmos. Even those religions that are basically creationist (Judaism, Christianity, Islam) have liberal wings committed to evolutionism, which now dominate the teaching in most main-line seminaries and religious colleges.

Not only is evolutionary philosophy basic in most anti-Christian social, economic, and religious philosophies, but it is also the pseudo-scientific rationale of the host of antisocial immoral practices that are devastating the world today (abortion, the drug culture, homosexual activism, animalistic amorality, and so on). By the very fact of goodness and beauty in the world, it would seem that such a harmful and godless theory of origins as evolutionism could not possibly be true.

Of course, if science had actually *proved* evolution to be true, we would have to accept it no matter how much it contradicts the Bible and undermines the concepts of God and true morality. The fact is, however, that it also contradicts true science. All the real facts of science support special creation— not evolution. The evidence for this truth will be outlined in the remaining sections of this chapter.

THE ORIGIN OF LIFE

The theory of evolution has a fatal flaw right at the beginning: it is impossible to account for the origin of life in the first place. The popular notion of spontaneous generation was demolished by Louis Pasteur and others back in the nineteenth century, yet evolutionists still cling to the idea of "abiogenesis," the imaginary gradual development of complex molecules from basic elements until they finally become replicating molecules, which are then assumed to be living.

Despite much media-induced misunderstanding on this point, no replicating molecule has ever yet been synthesized from nonliving chemicals in the laboratory, despite multitudes of costly experiments attempting to do so. Yet evolutionists imagine that what cannot be accomplished by trained scientists with costly equipment in artificially-controlled environments somehow occurred by blind chance a billion years ago. Some unknown process operating in an unknown liquid mixture beneath an unknown type of atmosphere somehow generated unknown primitive life forms from unknown chemicals, and that's how life began!

However, life even at the simplest imaginary level is so complex that the chance for this to happen by accident is infinitesimally small. The famous mathematical astrophysicist, Sir Fred Hoyle, recently argued that the probability this could have happened even once in the entire history of the universe is roughly equivalent to the probability that a tornado sweeping through a junkyard would assemble a Boeing 747.

Living organisms are known to be structured around a

remarkable system called the DNA molecule (deoxyribonucleic acid), in which is encoded all the information necessary to direct the growth of the complete organism from the germ cell. Although the variational potential in the DNA molecule is extremely large, allowing a wide range of variation in any given type of plant or animal, it also serves to insure that such variation will be within the fixed limits represented in the genetic systems of the parents. The tremendous amount of ordered information in even the simplest living organism is so great that it is almost impossible to imagine that scientists could ever synthesize it from elemental chemicals, no matter how long they took, and even more inconceivable that it could ever happen by chance.

Even if a genetic code centered in the DNA molecule could ever arise by chance, it certainly could never happen more than once. Yet it has recently been found that there are several *different* genetic codes present in certain organisms, and all evidence indicates that each must have had a separate origin.

The intensive search for even the slightest traces of life on other planets or in interplanetary space reflects the wistful hope that evolutionary theory will be vindicated by evidence that life has also developed somewhere else in the universe. As yet, despite the space probes, giant telescopes, and even the UFO furor, the idea of extraterrestrial life remains science fiction and nothing more. There is not the slightest evidence of biological life as we understand it anywhere else in the universe.

The fact that almost all living flesh is composed of the same basic type of molecule (DNA), made up in turn of the same basic elements (carbon, hydrogen, nitrogen, oxygen, and so on) found in the earth is of course a definite confirmation of Scripture. The Bible states plainly that both plants (Genesis 1:11–12) and animals (Genesis 1:20, 24) were "brought forth" from the earth and its waters, and that even man's body was formed of "the dust of the ground" (Genesis 2:7). However, the fact that there was a life principle that was not inherent in these basic substances is also stressed in the case of both animals ("living creatures," Genesis 1:24) and man ("living soul," 2:7), and there is not the slightest evidence that future scientists will ever be able to synthesize anything corresponding to a "living soul," nor that natural processes ever accomplished any such thing in the past.

Of course, from the standpoint of the evolutionists, it is necessary to postulate some form of spontaneous generation or abiogenesis, for otherwise they would have to assume a creator. Thus, they continue to believe in a naturalistic origin of life by sheer blind faith and against infinite odds, not by scientific evidence at all.

ORIGIN OF THE SPECIES

More than one hundred years ago, Charles Darwin achieved lasting fame by publishing *The Origin of the Species*. Yet it is now recognized that, in that book, he never gave one specific example of the origin of any new species of plant or animal. He discussed numerous examples of "variation" *within* species and indulged in many speculations as to how different organisms might have evolved in the past, along with various notions as to possible relationships deduced from similarities, but he never gave any real proof of genuine *vertical* evolution. Yet, his speculative theory of unlimited variation and gradual accumulation of favorable variations by natural selection was soon accepted the world over as proof that all things had come into being by evolution.

It is now known, of course, that all such Darwinian "variations" occur within fixed limits, following in general the mathematical laws of heredity described by Darwin's contemporary, Gregor Mendel. Numerous types of "genes," controlling in a complex and not-yet-understood way the various physical characteristics of the organism, can combine and "recombine" in various ways to generate a great variety of individual features, so that no two individuals are ever exactly alike. This process is not "evolution," however—merely *variation*—and creationists regard this process as part of the creative plan of God. Not only does it account for the important phenomenon of individuality, but it also allows plants and animals to adapt to changing environments without becoming extinct. Mere variation, however, is nothing but *horizontal* change at the same level of organizational complexity, and it always seems to be confined within definite limits. There is no evidence whatever that such *limited horizontal* changes ever become the *unlimited vertical* changes required for real evolution to take place. "Microevolution," as some call this type of change, has no demonstrated connection with "macroevolution," at least as far as any actual physical evidence goes. Within all human history, there has never been documented one single example of any kind of organism evolving into a more complex kind of organism or even into a truly new "species" at the same level. By contrast, there have been thousands of examples of plants and animals that have become extinct during human history. If "the present is the key to the past," as naturalistic scientists like to imagine, then the universal law of biological science would seem to be deterioration and extinction rather than evolution.

It is significant that, even at this late date, well over a century after Darwin and despite the lifelong efforts of thousands of scientists and untold millions of dollars spent on elaborate studies and experiments, evolutionists still have never experimentally observed the evolution of a single new species, nor do they have any certain knowledge of the mechanism by which evolution works. This is an amazing situation for a phenomenon that is widely promoted as one of the verities of modern science. There is certainly no parallel to this situation anywhere else in science.

As to evolutionary mechanisms, there has been no dearth of suggestions. Among the more prominent have been the acquired characteristics theory of Lamarck, the Darwinian theory of natural selection, the mutation theory of De Vries, various theories of vitalistic orthogenesis (emergent evolution, nomogenesis, and so on), various "saltational" theories (e.g., Goldschmidt's "hopeful monster" theory), and finally the currently competing theories (as of 1986) of neo-Darwinism (or the "modern evolutionary synthesis," as constructed by such men as Julian Huxley, Ernst Mayr, George Gaylord Simpson, and Theodosius Dobzhansky) and the still-more-recent theory of "punctuated equilibrium" (vigorously promoted by Niles Eldredge, Stephen Jay Gould, and many of the younger school of "revolutionary evolutionists").

There is neither the space nor the need to discuss any of these or other evolutionary theories in detail here. The significant point is their variety and the intense intra-establishment quarreling among their respective proponents. It is clear that no one has yet acquired any understanding of how evolution really works.

It is known, of course, that distinctly new characteristics can be generated in a plant or animal by the phenomenon of mutation. Variations represent mere recombinations of genetic factors already present, whereas mutations seem to involve something altogether new. An accumulation of beneficial mutations, preserved in the population by the phenomenon of natural selection, could then in principle eventually develop new species, so the argument goes.

The problem is that there are no *beneficial* mutations. All *known* mutations so far have been either lethal, harmful, neutral, or even reversible. In terms of the "genetic code," a mutation is essentially a "mistake" in transmission of hereditary information caused by one or more random changes in the DNA molecular structure. Most laboratory mutations have been induced artificially by chemicals, heat, radiation, or other such disturbing influences. Otherwise, mutations in nature are quite rare, and, when they do occur, they usually tend to disappear rather quickly, being neutral or pathologic rather than helpful in the assumed "struggle for existence." If they survive at all, they build up a "genetic load" in the population, reducing its over-all viability. Evolutionists continue to *believe* in beneficial mutations (they almost have to in order to believe in evolution), but they never *see* any. The few that are occasionally cited (e.g., the color change in the peppered moth and the resistance to DDT developed by certain insects) have, of course, long since been recognized by geneticists as mere recombinations of genetic factors already present—not true mutations at all. Some so-called mutations are predictable or even reversible, but these could just as well be considered a form of recombination.

The reason that actual mutations are harmful is simply because they represent *random* restructuring of the very complex, highly organized replicating systems of the living cell. When *any* complex system undergoes a random change, it will become *less* organized and therefore less functional. Increased organization requires an input of organizing information, not a random reshuffling caused by the entrance of an extraneous force from outside (like, say, a tornado in a junkyard or a bull in a china shop).

Mutations may contribute to extinction of the species or to deterioration of the species, but it is impossible to see how they could ever bring about the origin of species. It is no wonder, therefore, that evolutionists have never been able to see new species evolve, or that they have never been able to find any mechanism by which evolution might work.

CIRCUMSTANTIAL EVIDENCES

The fact that most biologists continue to believe in evolution, despite the massively negative experimental evidence, is presumably because of certain circumstantial evidences that they cite in support of it.

Similarities between organisms (homologies) are appealed to, for one thing. Resemblances between different species are

analyzed in terms of comparative anatomy, comparative embryology, comparative biochemistry, comparative behaviors, and
other such factors and then used to measure the hypothetical
closeness of ancestral relationships. The fact that men and apes
have certain features in common, for example, is supposed to
indicate that they have a common ancestor. The general classification system (species, genera, families, orders, classes, phyla,
kingdoms) that has been set up to distinguish different kinds of
plants and animals is assumed then to correspond approximately
to an actual family tree representing the evolutionary ancestry of
all organisms.

But this type of evidence is evidence of nothing whatever
except the ability of its inventor to arrange a conglomeration of
objects into "nested" objects of similar sizes and shapes. One
could do the same thing with the automobiles on a used-car lot
or the tools in a machine shop or any other collection of similar
but heterogeneous objects.

As a matter of fact, the structural and physiological
differences between organisms are more significant than their
similarities. If all organisms really had a common ancestor,
there should be a *continuity* between them rather than clear-cut
gaps. It should not even be possible to arrange a classification
system at all. One could never tell where the "cats" stop and
the "dogs" begin with all the intermediate "dats" and "cogs"
running around. Where did the differences come from?

These special differences, of course, are best explained by
special creation. Similarities and homologies *might* be attributable to evolution from a common ancestor, but they are even
better explained in terms of creation by a common Designer.
Thus, similarities and differences as a whole constitute powerful
evidence for special creation, with similar structures created for
similar functions and different structures for different functions,
all planned in accord with the creative handiwork of an omni-
scient Creator. *Every* normal structure in *every* organism is

evidence of design for a specific purpose and cannot be explained by chance.

The old circumstantial argument from vestigial organs is still mentioned occasionally in evolutionary textbooks. According to this idea, certain supposedly useless organs in man (tonsils, appendix, coccyx, and so on) are atrophied vestiges of useful organs in certain of man's animal ancestors. At one time, there were supposed to be 180 such vestigial organs in man. The list is now itself a vestige, with almost all of its entries gradually deleted as medical science discovered the very essential physiological roles still being played by these "useless" organs. However, a similar argument is now being advanced by modern advocates of the punctuated-equilibrium concept, to the effect that evolution is not evidenced by the beautiful "adaptations" in nature (these can be better explained by creative design, as noted above) but by nature's "imperfections"—that is, organs that don't work as well as they could if they were better designed.

This type of argument has been advanced by S. J. Gould and other punctuationists who would play down the role of gradual evolution by natural selection, with survival of the fittest, or best adapted, in favor of the more sudden, random changes suggested by nature's "gaps" and discontinuities. However, this argument from imperfections, like the argument from vestigial organs, is nothing but unconfessed ignorance of their real functions. Furthermore, if there *are* any vestigial organs or imperfect adaptations in nature, they are better explained as evidence of deterioration rather than improvement, just as mutations are.

Another important circumstantial evidence offered for evolution, at least when the theory first was being developed in its modern form, was the recapitulation theory, which taught that "ontogeny recapitulates phylogeny"—that is, that the embryologic development of any organism was a condensed recapitulation of the past evolutionary development of that organism. This theory, first vigorously advocated in Germany by Ernst Haeckel (whose philosophy greatly influenced Adolf Hitler toward pantheism, racism, and imperialism), has been thoroughly discredited scientifically by modern embryologists but is still widely believed. Its application in science has wrought untold harm for more than a hundred years.

In the first place, it spawned much embryological study for the purpose of building up supposed evolutionary histories for different kinds of animals, and from them, fossil sequences that later would constitute the geologic column. This fossil "record" originally built up, not from actual field evidence in paleontology but mostly from studies of comparative embryology and morphology, is often now presented as the main "evidence" for evolution. The fossil evidence will be discussed shortly in more detail, but its questionable background via the falsified theory of recapitulation is worth noting here.

Another bitter fruit of the recapitulation theory was its use as a supposed scientific justification for racism and abortion. Each human embryo was alleged by Haeckel and his followers to be repeating the evolutionary history of its ancestors, starting as a one-celled organism in a liquid environment, then becoming a multicelled invertebrate, then a fish with gill slits, later a monkey with a tail, and eventually a human being. Even then, the story was not finished, as a Caucasian human infant had to develop through stages corresponding to the "lower" human races (hence, the origin of the term "mongolism") before becoming a full-fledged member of the "master" race.

As bizarre as such ideas may appear to us today, this sort of thinking was common among nineteenth-century evolutionary scientists. Not only Haeckel but a whole generation of these scientists, including Darwin and his "bulldog," Thomas Huxley, were white racists, and they used evolutionary philosophy to justify their position. As far as the modern abortion epidemic is concerned, whenever anyone tries to offer a scientific rationale for this practice today, it is on the premise that the fetus has not yet developed into its "human" stage; it is no great sin to kill a fish or a monkey. As a matter of fact, many people today seem more concerned about the lives of monkeys or other animals than those of unborn children.

The fact is, of course, that *every* stage in the development of every embryo that has been so studied is necessary to the most efficient development of that particular kind of creature. The marvelous embryonic growth of all living creatures at every step, instead of supporting evolution, is actually testimony to a Designer and Creator.

THE FOSSIL RECORD

Most evolutionists believe that fossils provide the best evidence for evolution, even though it is also a strictly circumstantial type of evidence. Evolutionists generally admit, as we have seen, that there is no evidence whatever that "vertical" evolution is occurring at present, so they argue that this type of evolution (that is, *real* evolution—macroevolution) requires millions of years. So they claim that evolution has occurred in the past, even though it progresses too slowly to be seen in the present. For evidence of that, they must appeal to the fossil record.

The fossil remains of formerly living plants and animals are found in great numbers in the sedimentary rocks of the earth's crust. These have been organized into a standard "geologic column," representing the various supposed geological ages of the past. In this standard column, only simple and unspecialized forms of life are found in the lower strata (therefore, the "older" ages). Then, as the surface is approached, increasingly high and complex types appear. This gradual increase in size and complexity of the fossils has, in fact, served as the main basis of identifying the various geologic strata and correlating them from place to place. The time during which these strata have been deposited is believed to extend over hundreds of millions of years. All of this is considered to be strong evidence that evolution *has* occurred in the past, even though we cannot see it occurring in the present.

There are a number of serious difficulties with this geological time scale and the evolutionary interpretation of its fossil record. Some of these problems will be considered in the next chapter, and a different interpretation will be suggested. However, if we temporarily assume that the geological ages actually occurred and the geological time scale is trustworthy, there are still several important facts in the fossil record that argue convincingly against evolution.

In the first place, out of the billions of fossils that have been shown to exist in the mile-deep graveyard extending around the earth, there are no fossils of true evolutionary transitional forms. Every one of the great phyla, orders, classes, and families, as well as most genera and species, appear quite suddenly in the fossil record, with no preliminary or intermediate forms leading up to them. This has long been a serious problem for those evolutionists who take such data seriously, not merely attributing them to the "incompleteness" of the fossil record. It is the main reason for the sudden popularity of the current "punctuated equilibrium" theory, which has been developed in an attempt to provide a rationale for these universal gaps in the fossil record. There are no transitional sequences from one species to another species, let alone transitions between genera, families, and higher categories in the classification scheme.

This is a strange situation if evolution really took place in the past. It is reasonable to expect that, out of the multitudes of fossils that *have* been preserved, at least a few should have been found with transitional features. This follows directly from statistical sampling theory. It seems necessary to conclude, therefore, that the real reason transitional fossils have never been found is because transitional animals never existed.

A second problem is that many species—not to mention genera and the higher categories—have remained essentially unchanged throughout all the supposed geological ages since they first appeared. Even more of these unchanged forms would be recognized except for the practice that paleontologists have of giving new names to fossilized species regardless of how closely they resemble living species. Among the creatures that have remained unchanged throughout the course of evolutionary history are the very protozoa with which evolution is supposed to have begun. This is difficult to understand if evolutionary change actually is the universal law of nature.

A third problem in reference to the fossil record is that a great many modern kinds of animals are evidently degenerate, rather than higher, forms of those that are found as fossils. These would include practically all mammals—elephants, tigers, wolves, rhino, hippos, bears, beavers, and others. It is also true of multitudes of plants of all kinds, as well as insects (giant ants, giant cockroaches, giant dragonflies, and so on), birds, fish, amphibians, and reptiles.

SUPPOSED TRANSITIONAL FOSSILS

There have been, however, a few well-publicized fossils that are occasionally cited as possible transitional forms. These require a closer look. The most frequently cited example is *Archaeopteryx,* the supposed half-reptile/half-bird that is supposed to prove that reptiles evolved into birds. This peculiar creature seems to have had teeth and claws like a reptile and wings and feathers like a bird.

However, at the very most, *Archaeopteryx* was a "mosaic" form, not a transitional form. That is, each of its attributes was fully developed and functional, not incipient or atrophying. Its wings and feathers were complete and perfect, not half-legs or half-scales in the process of evolving into wings and feathers.

Furthermore, fossils of true birds have been found in strata at least as "old" as those in which *Archaeopteryx* fossils have been found, so that the latter, whatever it was, could not have been the "first bird" as evolutionists have claimed. Still further, in 1984, a number of leading scientists found significant evidence that the only two complete *Archaeopteryx* fossils had been artificially constructed and "planted" by a clever hoaxer shortly after the publication of Darwin's *Origin of Species*. At this writing (1986) this possibility is still under investigation, but even if *Archaeopteryx* was a real animal, it was simply a toothed bird, now extinct, just like dinosaurs and pterodactyls. It was not an evolutionary transition at all.

There is also the famous horse series, which is supposed to show the gradual evolution of the horse from a small three-toed animal, *Eohippus*, through several intermediate stages to the modern, large, one-toed horse, *Equus*. This "series" is a common museum and textbook illustration of evolution.

The fact is, however, that this supposed series is quite artificial, with the chronological relationships between its members resembling a bush more than a tree or ladder. All these animals are said to have lived in the Tertiary period, late in geologic time. They are found near the surface, in the relatively unconsolidated Tertiary deposits. The different forms are not found superimposed over one another but at widely separated localities, sometimes continents apart. No gradual transitions are evident between the different forms with transitional structural features but only sudden jumps at best. The different supposed evolutionary stages of the horse in many cases overlap each other in their respective geological "ages," and yet there are no transitions (i.e., with transitional, half-developed structures) between any two of these stages.

At the very most, this assumed horse pedigree would not involve major changes but only variation within the biological family of the horses. There is a possibility that, in some cases at least, the created "kind" of Genesis may correspond to the family. Within each kind, God has created a genetic system that allows a wide range of *horizontal* variation, enabling the particular kind to adapt to a wide range of environments. This is not evolution, however, since there is no *vertical* change toward a different, more complex kind.

In the case of the "horses," all are quite similar to each other with the exception of *Eohippus,* the so-called "dawn horse," and this animal should probably not even be included in the series at all. The original name assigned to *Eohippus* was *Hyracotherium* because of its obvious similarity to the modern animal called the hyrax. This name has now come into common use again, and it is probable that *Eohippus* is really an extinct variety of hyrax, with no genealogical connection to the horse at all.

Thus, with the exception of *Hyracotherium,* who was probably a hyrax, or at least a separate now-extinct animal, it seems plausible to say that each of the several horse genera (*Pliohippus, Merychippus,* and so on) may have been living simultaneously, perhaps as variants of the originally created horse kind, and that they, in common with many other zoological inhabitants of a former age, have since become extinct.

Even if one of these forms turns out to be the ancestor of the modern *Equus* (and this is not yet proved, by any means), the loss of one or more toes is hardly an advance. In common with other known mutations, this is a deterioration, giving no information as to how the three or four toes evolved in the first place. The variant sizes are irrelevant, as there are both midget horses and giant horses living today, all interfertile.

Similar objections could be lodged against the so-called evolutionary pedigrees of the camel, the elephant, and other animals. Other supposed fossil transitional forms, such as the mammal-like reptiles, were successful mosaic forms; not transitional forms, each with no known evolutionary connection either to any reptile or to any mammal or to any of the other mammal-like reptiles.

THE APE-MEN

There still remains the problem of the fossils that have been classed as ape-human intermediates, the "hominid" forms. The evolutionary reconstructions one sees in museums and textbooks sometimes seem quite impressive, but they are highly imaginative and speculative.

The fossils of these supposed hominids are fragmentary and questionable. Since many fossils of true apes and true men have been found, the very scarcity of fossils that could even be consided as possible intermediate forms between apes and men is alone enough to discredit the theory of man's apelike ancestry. Only a few bone fragments have been found that have been imaginatively construed as some sort of lower species of man. This is a strange situation in view of the multiplied millions of "ape-men" that must have lived and died during the hypothetical million-year transition from the first apelike ancestor to man.

The few fossils offered as evidence by paleoanthropologists have mostly been discredited by evolutionary anthropologists themselves. The three hominids that were being promoted most vigorously by evolutionists when I was going to college were Java man, Peking man, and Piltdown man. The bones of the original Java man *(Pithecanthropus erectus)* have since been recognized as belonging to two different creatures—the skull to a gibbon, the femur to a man. The fossils of the original Peking man were quite controversial from the beginning but in any case were lost during World War II. Piltdown man, of course, is now universally acknowledged to be a hoax—but a hoax that fooled the world's leading anthropologists for decades.

Other fossils considered in the same category as these, however, have been found later and are now generally grouped in a genus named *Homo erectus*. These have all been very incomplete skeletons, however, and their chronology also is doubtful. The most nearly complete such skeleton thus far was found in Kenya and announced to the public only in 1985. Its aspect was distinctly human in size and posture, and even the skull looked much like that of Neanderthal man, except for its relatively small cranial capacity. The latter, together with its supposed great antiquity, was supposed to have required a *Homo erectus* identification. However, while it is true that the skull size was smaller than the 1,500 cubic centimeter average of modern *Homo sapiens,* it was nevertheless within the range of the latter, so might very well have been from a true human being. As far as the dating of *Homo erectus* is concerned, certain of these fossils have been dated as recent, within the time of modern man; others have been dated as very old, at least as old as many fossils of *Australopithecus,* a supposed ancestor of *Homo erectus.* In any case, *Homo erectus* is acknowledged to be in the same genus as modern *Homo sapiens,* and at least some of these specimens were probably no more different from modern man than modern men are from each other.

In recent years great attention has been centered on *Australopithecus,* a supposed hominid represented by a number of fossils found in South Africa by Raymond Dart, Louis Leakey, Richard Leakey, Carl Johanson, and others. Anthropologists have been bitterly divided over the evolutionary status of these australopithecines. Some think they were practically identical with the modern pygmy chimpanzee; some think they were erect walkers, while others insist they were knuckle-walkers or tree-swingers. Their chronology overlaps with that of *Homo erectus.* Some are convinced that these were the direct apelike ancestors of modern man, whereas others argue that they were true apes that in turn were descended from a manlike ancestor. The famous footprints found by Mary Leakey in Tanzania have been attributed to *Australopithecus,* but they were virtually identical with modern human footprints and probably were not made by *Australopithecus* at all. At best, the status of *Australopithecus* is equivocal, but the high probability is that this creature was an extinct ape, with no evolutionary relation to man.

The past sixty or so years have even witnessed a number of noteworthy scientific blunders by evolutionists. In addition to the famous Piltdown hoax, there was the case of *Hesperopithecus*, a tooth found in 1922 in Nebraska and promoted by Henry Fairfield Osborn of the American Museum of Natural History as an ape-man. Osborn was even ready to introduce it at the 1925 Scopes trial as evidence for human evolution. Two years later, however, the complete skeleton was found, and it proved to have belonged to an extinct pig. There have been many other such instances, but they have all been ignored and quickly forgotten by evolutionists.

The Neanderthal and Cro-Magnon tribes of cavemen were originally thought to be ape-men but are now universally accepted as true men, *Homo sapiens*. A number of fossils of men have also been found in ancient strata, supposedly laid down before man evolved. These include the Calaveras skull, Petralona man, the Wadjak skulls, Castenodolo and Olno skulls, and others, but evolutionists commonly try to explain these away as hoaxes, geologically reworked, or by various other devices.

In view of the chaotic state of modern paleoanthropology, there is nothing to refute the creationist point of view that apes were created as apes and people as people. Many of the supposed "hominid" fossils (e.g., *Australopithecus, Ramapithecus*) *are* extinct apes, where others (e.g., Neanderthal) clearly represent extinct tribes of men. Such extinct tribes, or "races," as some would call them, are best explained as descendants of families that emigrated from Babel after the "confusion of tongues." As a result of isolation, inbreeding, and (perhaps) mutations, they gradually deteriorated in strength and intelligence and eventually became extinct.

EVOLUTION VERSUS ENTROPY

These indications add emphasis to a principle already alluded to several times, namely, that deterioration or degeneration rather than developmental evolution is the universal law of biology. As we have seen, there is *no* real evidence at all for progressive evolution but much evidence for disintegration and extinction or, at best, biologic stability.

We have already seen in the previous chapter that this law of degeneration, or entropy increase, is universally operative throughout the physical and chemical realms; it now seems also to pervade the biologic realm. In fact, this truth is beginning so to disturb evolutionists that a number of books and papers have been published in recent years attempting to "harmonize" the concept of evolution (increasing complexity) with the entropy principle (decreasing complexity).

These attempts have been futile. It is not possible to equate deterioration with development. Evolution and entropy are both supposed to represent universal laws of change, but each is the opposite of the other, so they cannot both be true. Entropy represents a *law of science,* to the extent there is such a thing, whereas evolution represents the wishful thinking of those trying to explain the existence of life apart from God and has no scientific basis at all.

More and more it appears that there is a degenerative principle pervading all nature. Some have called this the "law of morpholysis" (which means "breaking-down of structure"), but the Bible explains it as the great curse placed on the ground because of Adam's sin (Genesis 3:17–20). According to this principle, "the whole creation groaneth and travaileth in pain together until now" under "the bondage of corruption (or 'decay')" (Romans 8:22, 21). There is a universal tendency from the highly organized to the disorganized. Never is there an inherent, natural, undirected, unaided trend toward an increase of organized complexity. The natural tendency is always degenerative. Prior to the curse, entropy, like energy, was "conserved" with decay processes balanced by growth processes. Now, however, decay prevails.

In biology, an important example is found in the agencies supposed to bring about evolution; that is, gene mutations. All such changes are harmful (or neutral at best), because they represent a breaking down of the highly structured arrangement of the genes in the germ cell. This most likely accounts for the fact that most of the living creatures of the present are represented in the fossil record of the past by larger, more highly developed members of the same kind. It probably also accounts for the extinction of many former kinds of living things, as well as for the various "imperfect adaptations" and "vestigial organs" (to the extent there really are any such imperfections and vestiges), which evolutionists still cite (unrealistically) as evidence for evolution.

Evolutionists still may insist that the law of increasing entropy does not preclude evolution since biological systems are "open" systems and can draw enough energy from the sun to support an upward evolution. That is nonsense, however, since the equations of thermodynamics clearly show that an influx of raw heat energy (as from the sun) into any open system (say, like the earth) will increase the entropy (or decay) of that system more rapidly than if it were an isolated system.

Under certain special conditions (not available to evolution, as far as all evidence goes), the organization of an open system may be increased for a time by the entrance of external *ordering* energy, or information. Examples would be the growth of a plant from a seed or the construction of a building from various structural components. Any such growth process, however, must have a directing program (such as the genetic code in the DNA of the seed or the blueprint for the building), as well as an energy conversion mechanism of some sort to convert the raw energy of the solar heat into the specific work of building up the structure (such as the amazingly complex mechanism of photosynthesis for the seed, or the machinery, fuels, muscles, and minds of the builders in the case of the building). The imaginary evolutionary growth of complex plants and animals from a primeval cell (and *that* from nonliving chemicals in a hypothetical primordial soup), however, has neither a directing program nor conversion mechanism to accomplish this. It must rely on time and chance, but time and chance break things down—they don't build them up.

No one has ever seen anything evolve, no one knows how evolution works, the fossil record shows no evolutionary transitions taking place, and the basic laws of science show it to be impossible. Yet evolutionists insist that *this* is "science" and should be taught as proved fact to schoolchildren.

3

Science and the Flood

In Genesis 6–9 appears the record of the great global cataclysm known as the Noahic Flood. All men, as well as all land animals except those in Noah's ark, were destroyed by a great world-enveloping flood that was sent as divine punishment because "all flesh had corrupted his way upon the earth" (Genesis 6:12).

The biblical record describes a great flood that inundated and devastated the entire earth. Some writers, because of what they feel are insuperable geological and archaeological difficulties with the global-flood record, have tried to interpret the record as either a "local flood" or, in some cases, as a universal "tranquil flood." Most critics of the Bible have dismissed the entire record as purely legendary.

THE FLOOD—A GLOBAL CATACLYSM

However, if the Bible is allowed to speak for itself, an unprejudiced reader must understand the writer of the account to be describing a worldwide flood. Consider such passages as the following:

> I . . . do bring a flood of waters upon the earth, to destroy all flesh, wherein is the breath of life, from under heaven; and every thing that is in the earth shall die. (Genesis 6:17)

> Every living substance that I have made will I destroy from off the face of the earth. (Genesus 7:4)

> And the waters prevailed exceedingly upon the earth; and all the high hills, that were under the whole heaven, were covered. Fifteen cubits upward did the waters prevail; and the mountains were covered. (Genesis 7:19–20)

> And every living substance was destroyed which was upon the face of the ground, both man, and cattle, and the creeping things, and the fowl of the heaven; and they were destroyed from the earth: and Noah only remained alive, and they that were with him in the ark. (Genesis 7:23)

> And I will establish my covenant with you; neither shall all flesh be cut off any more by the waters of a flood; neither shall there be any more a flood to destroy the earth. (Genesis 9:11)

There are at least thirty such expressions of cataclysmic universality in the biblical record of the Flood, and those theologians who try to explain the event as a local flood or a tranquil flood thereby forfeit all right to be recognized as reliable expositors of the Word of God, no matter how prestigious they might seem to be in the academic or religious worlds. Biblical references to the Flood are not limited to the early chapters of Genesis but also occur frequently in later parts of the Bible (Psalm 29:1–11; 104:5–9; Isaiah 54:9; Matthew 24:37–39; Luke 17:26–27; Hebrews 11:7; 1 Peter 3:19–20; 2 Peter 2:5; 3:3–6; and so on), and all those passages can only be understood in the context of a universal Flood.

Even if only the mountains in the immediate vicinity of the

mountains of Ararat on which the ark grounded when the waters began to recede after 150 days of rising (Genesis 7:24—8:5) were covered, it would not have been possible for the floodwaters to be retained in the local vicinity. The present Mount Ararat is seventeen thousand feet high, and it was two-and-a-half months after the ark grounded before the tops of *any* mountains could even be seen. It was an additional 4½ months before the water level went down enough to let the occupants leave the ark. To imagine that a year-long, seventeen-thousand-foot high flood could have been a *local* flood is absurd.

The story of the Flood becomes a silly fable if it is interpreted as a local event. The elaborate provisions for the preservation of life in the ark were utterly unnecessary. God could merely have warned Noah to move into a nearby region that the Flood would not cover, and Noah could have done that with far less time and labor than were needed for the construction of the ark and the collection of the animals and birds. Finally, if the Genesis Flood was only local, then God's promise that there would never again be such a flood was a lie. In the writer's commentary on Genesis (*The Genesis Record,* Baker, 1976), an appendix lists 100 reasons, both biblical and scientific, for accepting the Genesis Flood as a worldwide cataclysm. Even less defensible is the idea of a worldwide tranquil flood. A worldwide tranquil flood is about as physically plausible as a worldwide tranquil explosion. The concept is a contradiction in terms.

It has been necessary to stress the universality of the cataclysmic Flood as taught in the inspired word of God, because that fact does have profound scientific consequences, especially in the fields of historical geology and archaeology. The biblical record shows that the physical cause of the Flood was both atmospheric ("windows of heaven opened") and geophysical ("fountains of the great deep broken up"). Such a gigantic catastrophe must have profoundly changed the geographic and stratigraphic features of the earth's surface as it then was, making it almost impossible now to discern geologically with any degree of assurance those things that may have taken place in the earth before the Flood. The evolutionary interpretation of the fossil record would have to be abandoned, with the sedimentary rocks and their fossiliferous contents reinterpreted in terms of the great hydraulic cataclysm. And if the fossils do not give evidence of evolution, there remains *no* evidence that life has evolved at all.

Consequently and of necessity, those who are committed to belief in evolution *must* maintain that the worldwide Flood described in the Bible never took place—in spite of the overwhelming ethnological, philological, archaeological, and geological evidence that it *did* take place. And those theological "intellectuals" who believe that Christians must at all costs maintain favor with evolutionary intellectuals are thereby forced to promote interpretations such as the local flood or the tranquil flood theories.

THE STANDARD SYSTEM OF HISTORICAL GEOLOGY

The basic creed of historical geology ever since the days of Hutton and Lyell in the early nineteenth century has been *uniformitarianism,* summarized in the motto: "The present is the key to the past." This is the assumption that all observable systems, both living and nonliving, can be explained as to origin and development in terms of purely natural laws and with processes operating at essentially modern rates. As applied to geology, this means that all the earth's mountains, rivers, huge stratigraphic deposits—in short, all features of the earth's crust and surface—are explainable as the result of the slow processes of sedimentation, erosion, contraction, radioactivity, and other actions of natural processes all working over almost infinitely long periods of time. It is assumed to be "unscientific" to use unnatural events such as creation or the Flood to explain any of these phenomena.

The idea of slow processes and infinite ages was all but

universally held among the pagan nations of antiquity. With the Renaissance and Reformation, however, and especially with the great increase in Bible reading that followed the invention of the printing press and the religious revivals associated with Protestantism and, later, the Great Awakening, the dominant theory of geology became Flood geology, the belief that all the fossil-bearing rock strata had been deposited in the Noahic Flood. That concept was expounded in the writings of Steno, the "father of stratigraphy," Woodward, the "father of paleontology," and other great geologists of the seventeenth and eighteenth centuries.

Gradually, the old pagan ideas were revived in modern garb, however, especially by Sir Charles Lyell (the "father of uniformitarianism"), then by Charles Darwin, and, by the end of the nineteenth century, practically the entire intellectual world had reverted to the ancient pagan, pantheistic beliefs in evolution and infinite ages, or what might be called "evolutionary uniformitarianism."

The "geologic time scale" worked out by Lyell and others (in western Europe and, to some extent, in New York) at that time has been standard ever since. This time scale is supposed to represent the "standard geologic column," the vertical cross section of sedimentary rocks and fossils now found in the earth's crust. It is built around four great assumed "eras" (in ascending order: Proterozoic, Paleozoic, Mesozoic, and Cenozoic) that are subdivided into twelve "periods" (Precambrian, Cambrian, Ordovician, Silurian, Devonian, Carboniferous, Permian, Triassic, Jurassic, Cretaceous, Tertiary, and Quaternary), with those in turn being further subdivided into "epochs."

Primitive one-celled organisms are supposed to have evolved in the Precambrian and all the animal phyla in the Cambrian, including even the vertebrates. The Mesozoic era was the age of the great reptiles, with birds and mammals proliferating in the Tertiary period. Man is supposed to have evolved in the Pleistocene epoch of the Quaternary period, or possibly in the

Pliocene epoch of the later Tertiary. Other details can be found in any standard textbook on geology, biology, or evolution.

All these "geological ages" had been worked out in considerable detail long before the discovery of radioactivity, so it is certainly incorrect for people to say that they have been determined by radiometric methods. As a matter of fact, much of the system was worked out even before many fossils were available. It was simply assumed—even by many theologians—that hierarchies of animal life should always move from simple to complex, from amoeba to man, and that this series should always be the same. Consequently, the data of comparative morphology (as formalized in the Linnaean classification system) and of comparative embryology (especially as expressed in Haeckel's now-discredited "recapitulation theory") were used to determine the sequences in which fossil series should be placed, even before such series were ever found in the rocks. Thus the geologic column, or "time-scale," is essentially an artificial construct based mainly on the assumption that the relative complexities of animal morphologies and the assumed evolutionary recapitulation in the growth of animal embryos should be mirrored in the fossil remains of organisms representing the advancing geological ages in earth's history. To considerable degree, this sytem was developed by "progressive creationists" such as Georges Cuvier and others (Cuvier was a leader in both comparative anatomy and paleontology), who were not themselves evolutionists but who believed in long ages and an ascending hierarchy of creation acts by God, rather than in the biblical record *per se*.

FALLACIES IN THE GEOLOGIC COLUMN

It is not surprising that a system constructed in such a strange and arbitrary manner should contain many anomalies and contradictions. One would gather from the typical textbook that the geologic column is found in complete and proper order everywhere in the world. The fact is that it exists *nowhere* in the real world, except on the pages of textbooks. The standard column is at least one hundred miles in thickness, whereas actual local columns average only a mile in thickness. Nowhere in the world is the complete column found; only a few of the twelve periods are normally found at any given location, and there are many places where *none* of the periods are found, with the crystalline "basement rocks" practically at the surface.

Furthermore, there is no correlation of rock characteristics as such with the "age" of the rocks. Any rock type (sandstone, shale, and so on) can be found in any age. Minerals of all types, metals of all types, coal and oil, structures of all types, and all degrees of looseness or consolidation can be found in any geological age.

How, then, is the age of a rock determined? The remarkable fact is that the geological age of a rock is determined primarily by the fossils it contains, on the basis of the fossil sequences that had been assigned to the different ages by Cuvier, Lyell, and their followers well over a century ago.

The circle of reasoning involved is subtle but once assumed generates a powerful argument for evolution. The fact of evolution (i.e., the assumed ladder of progress from simple to complex) is assumed in building up the geological series; rocks containing simpler fossils are older and rocks containing more complex and specialized forms are called younger. Then, the paleontological sequences so constructed are taken as proof of evolution. The main evidence for evolution (the fossil record) is based on the assumption of evolution implicit in the dating of the rocks by the fossils in the record.

However, in spite of the fact that the whole system is based on circular reasoning, it still contains many anomalies and contradictions. It is realistic to say that, at various specific locations around the world, one can find local geologic columns containing just about any combination of formations representing any number of periods in any chronological order. Many locations exhibit "young" formations resting conformably (i.e., with the strata above parallel to those below) on "old" formations, with many intermediate "ages" missing. Often such missing periods are not at all evident, with the younger resting in perfect conformity on the older with no evidence of an interruption in the deposition process. Such cases are called disconformities or diastems or even deceptive conformities. In such cases, the only evidence that the ages are missing is that their "index fossils" are missing; otherwise, the beds would appear to have been deposited in quick succession, their strata all parallel and continuous.

Even more surprising to the uninitiated is the fact that the world is full of examples of strata occurring in the wrong evolutionary order, again often in perfect conformity. That is, great areas containing "old" fossils are found to rest perfectly naturally on rocks containing "young" fossils. Such inversions, on a small scale can, of course, be produced by local folding and faulting. Often, however, there is no physical evidence that vast beds extending over great areas came into their present positions by any other means than normal deposition. Evolutionists cannot admit *that*, however, without drastically modifying or abandoning their theory of evolution.

To avoid such action, uniformitarian geologists invented the auxiliary hypothesis of low-angle "thrust faults," or "overthrusts." In this scenario, great masses of rock have been severed from their original formations and somehow lifted up and shoved over on top of the adjacent areas, following which, surface erosion in subsequent ages removed the upper deposits, leaving only the older rocks lying on the younger ones beneath.

If any such things have ever happened, it must have involved an intense degree of catastrophism, quite inconsistent with the usual geological assumption of uniformitarianism. Ordinary gravity sliding would be impossible without complete disintegration of the rocks on one or both sides of the thrust fault. Floating by "geostatic" fluid pressures has been suggested, but it would be impossible to maintain such pressures long enough over such vast areas to do that without the pressures being lost by cracks developing in the moving rocks.

Nevertheless, scores of examples of this upside-down phenomenon exist all over the world. The famous "Lewis Overthrust" in Montana and Alberta, including all of the Glacier National Park, has fossils of the Paleozoic era overlying those of the Cretaceous. In Tennessee and Georgia a great "fault" running for hundreds of miles consists of Cambrian deposits resting quite normally on Carboniferous. In fact, the whole Appalachian region consists of great thicknesses of Paleozoic rocks on top of much "younger" beds. In the Rockies, there are the extensive Bannock, Heart Mountain, and other low-angle thrust faults. Much of the Swiss Alpine region (even the famous Matterhorn) is in this upside-down condition. The same is true of the Scottish highlands and the mountains of India. One of the "displacements" in China has been followed for more than 500 miles. A similar area of 85,000 square miles is known in Scandinavia. Every part of the world yields other examples. The "geologic column," as worked out in England, Paris, and New York, has not worked so well in other parts of the world.

Furthermore, many locations have fossils supposedly representing different "ages" in the same formation, so that the assumed chronological "ranges" of animals are continually having to be extended. All the animal phyla, including even the vertebrates, are now known to have lived in the most "ancient" period, the Cambrian. Many of the one-celled organisms of the Precambrian (including the famous *E-Coli* bacteria, commonly used in modern research) are still alive and well, and there is a rapidly growing list of "living fossils"—animals or plants supposedly extinct for many geological periods that suddenly turn up still living in the modern world. All kinds of anomalies are repeatedly encountered in the geological column.

In fact, some leading modern geologists (e.g., Dr. David Raup of the University of Chicago and the Field Museum of

Natural History) are acknowledging now that there is *no certain order* of the fossils. That is, statistical analysis has shown that the fossil sequences actually found can be explained just as well by random deposition as by deposition in any given order of evolutionary progress. Other leading paleontologists (e.g., Stephen Jay Gould of Harvard) have lamented the fact that the fossil record exhibits no clear "vector of progress." And yet that record was constructed specifically to fit early nineteenth century ideas of the assumed progress in earth history.

In view of all the foregoing problems with the standard geologic column, it seems that geologists should at least be willing to consider another model, one not based on evolutionary uniformitarianism but on biblical creationism and catastrophism. The latter model was the one followed by the founding fathers of geology and paleontology and was never disproved. It was simply abandoned, as a sort of sacrifice to the temper of the times. Biblical skepticism was growing and the technological revolution had stimulated expansive ideas of "progress" and "development." Especially in western Europe and America the idea of survival of the fittest as contributing to ultimate progress for all took strong hold. It is now time to reevaluate the discarded—but never refuted—biblical "model" of historical geology.

THE FLOOD MODEL OF GEOLOGY

Even if the geological time scale is assumed to be substantially correct as far as the relative positions of the fossils in the various strata are concerned (and it is generally true that, in any local column, marine invertebrates tend to be preserved in the deeper strata, land vertebrates in the higher strata, and so on), the biblical Flood can account for the order of deposition at least as well as can the evolutionary uniformitarian model.

In the world before the Flood, there were different environments just as there are in the present world, and different groups of creatures lived in these different environments. Therefore, a great cataclysm of the kind described in the Bible would not be expected to pile all types of creatures together heterogeneously throughout the world. Rather, it would necessarily drown together, transport together, and deposit together the particular assemblages of creatures living together. Thus, two or more strata might be deposited quite simultaneously but contain different groups of future fossils because of their different sources, directions of transport, and ending locations.

On the other hand, evolutionary geology implies that only one assemblage of organisms was living at any one time, so that these organisms can be used to identify any rock strata formed during that age. Such is certainly not the case in the present world, however, which is supposedly assumed by uniformitarians to be "the key to the past."

The biblical deluge was both terrestrial and atmospheric in nature. Tremendous torrents of water poured from the skies all over the world for forty days and forty nights. At the same time, all "the fountains of the great deep" cleaved open, implying great subterranean and subaqueous disturbances, probably creating great tsunami waves and ejecting great amounts of juvenile water and magmatic materials on the earth.

Such a flood would necessarily tend to affect first and bury deepest the creatures inhabiting the deep oceans, then those in shallower waters. Then the waters and disturbed sediments would overtake the amphibians and land-bordering creatures. Above these would be buried swamp, marsh, and low river-flat creatures, especially reptiles. Higher mammals would usually be able to retreat from the rising waters to some extent but also would eventually be drowned and perhaps buried in the sediments. Finally, men and women, the chief object of the waters, would be overtaken and carried under.

There would be many exceptions, but there can be no doubt that this order would be the usual order of deposition and this, of course, is exactly the assumed evolutionary order that has been imposed on the fossil record. Thus, the fossil deposits do not represent the evolution of life over many ages but rather the destruction of life in one age, the world before the Flood. To the extent there is any real "order" in the fossils, that order does not represent evolutionary progression but rather ecological communities buried roughly in the order of increasing elevation of habitat.

Many other factors would modify this general arrangement, of course, depending on local circumstances. Some strata might be reworked and redeposited, especially as the lands rose and the floodwaters retreated at the end of the Flood. The processes of uplift of the still-plastic sediments would produce great faults and folds and would open fissures that might quickly become great canyons as the massive volumes of water rushed down to the sea.

In the process of depositing the successive strata of any given formation, with the same sources of sediment and prospective fossils, the factor of hydrodynamic sorting would work rapidly to sort the materials into objects of similar size, shape, and density. The simpler, denser, more streamlined organisms within a given kind would tend to settle out lower than the more complex, "advanced" individuals of that kind, thus giving a superficial appearance of evolution even within the boundaries of the formation.

This, of course, is only a bare outline of the probable geological activity of the deluge. Further geologic work would be accomplished during the centuries of "residual catastrophism" after the Flood. Continuing volcanic and tectonic activity, intense storms, even an Ice Age and possible continental splittings and collisions are reasonable possibilities that could be inferred for the post-Flood centuries from the tremendous disruption of the atmospheric and terrestrial equilibria that existed before the Flood.

In a book of this size, and in view of the almost infinite variety of local geologic phenomena occurring around the world, it is impossible to attempt a complete outline of the events of the Flood. A number of books listed in the bibliography give additional information, and there is still much research to do before answers can be given to all the questions that could be raised about the Flood and its geological effects. Nevertheless, the Flood model provides a good framework within which to solve these problems, and it already provides better answers than the traditional model of evolutionary uniformitarianism.

THE REVIVAL OF CATASTROPHISM

In fact, uniformitarianism has proved so inadequate as a geological dogma that there has recently developed among geologists a strong neo-catastrophist movement that is radically changing the study of earth history. This corresponds in many ways to the revival of saltationism (in the form of "punctuated equilibrium") among biologists and paleontologists. Many are even suggesting that the "quantum speciation" events in biology may be triggered in some way by the "catastrophic" events that occur in geological or astral processes.

Neither the punctuationists nor the neo-catastrophists, of course, are proposing a return either to creationism, in the first case, nor flood geology in the second. All these new ideas are being proposed in the context of atheistic evolutionism—even Marxist revolutionism in many cases—but at least they are realistically admitting that the traditional Darwinian gradualism and Lyellian uniformitarianism do not fit the facts of science.

Many leading modern geologists, for example, including Derek Ager, recent president of the British Geological Association; James Shea, editor of the *Journal of Geological Education*; Robert Dott, recent president of the Society of Economic Paleontologists and Mineralogists; Stephen Jay Gould, professor of geology at Harvard; David Raup, curator of geology at the Field Museum in Chicago; and many others are now urging, in effect, that practically *all* geologic formations and structures must have formed catastrophically. The traditional uniformitarian gradual-ism simply could never have produced them, no matter how old the earth might be.

For example, modern volcanoes could never have produced the volcanic terrains of the Pacific Northwest or many other parts of the world, not to mention the tremendous igneous intrusions that have produced the giant batholiths, dikes, sills, and so on. The slight earthquakes of the present cannot possibly account for the great faults that formed the Sierra Nevada or the Tetons. The peat bogs of the present are completely incommen-surate with the great coal beds and multiple coal seams of the world. The deep canyons and extensive alluvial fills in the valleys of the world could never have been formed by the present rivers trickling through them. Modern-day salt flats and saline lakes certainly could not ever produce great salt beds and domes such as abound deep in the earth. The same judgment can be pronounced about practically every type of deposit or feature in the earth's crust. The present is, most certainly, *not* the key to the past!

Creationists and flood geologists have, like myself, been pointing out these facts for many decades. It is noteworthy that geologists are finally admitting them, though in most cases for altogether different reasons.

Modern geologists still insist that the earth is very old and that natural processes have always prevailed, denying both cre-ation and the biblical Flood. Their "catastrophes" are all re-gional catastrophes, separated from each other by vast time spans when nothing much was happening. They insist that the sudden appearance of new kinds of creatures does not imply special creation but some unknown form of special evolution. They likewise insist that the multitude of evidences of catastro-phism in geology does not imply a single worldwide hydraulic cataclysm (especially not the Genesis Flood) but many individ-ual natural catastrophes with no connection to each other. Lots of local floods, volcanic outpourings, asteroid or meteorite collisions, and so on—but no worldwide judgment by God. The concept of divine judgment is profoundly offensive to the natural man, especially intellectuals.

The creationist, of course, argues that since all the evidence points to catastrophism, with every feature formed rapidly, there is no evidence for the millions of years arbitrarily inserted between the catastrophes. Science (meaning, literally, *knowledge*) should be based on what we *see,* not what we *don't see*. What we see in the geologic and paleontologic records of the past is *no* transitional forms and *no* evidence of great time spans in between the catastrophic events that formed all the geologic features of the earth. The reasonable conclusion is that no such transitional forms or long time spans ever existed.

FOSSIL GRAVEYARDS

One of the most obvious indications of catastrophism is the vast fossil graveyards in the sedimentary rock column, averaging a mile deep all around the globe. The very existence of fossils indicates rapid burial of the organisms, followed by rapid compaction of the sediments encasing them, else they would not have been preserved at all. Yet fossils are found everywhere by the billions. They have provided the supposed chief evidence for evolution, and they are the means by which geologists think they can determine the age of the rock in which they are found.

Fossil fish beds have been found that extend for miles, containing fish by the billions, in many places (Scotland, New York, California, Wyoming, and so on). Nothing like this is being formed today anywhere. Great dinosaur beds have been excavated in New Mexico, Alberta, Tanzania, Belgium, Spitzbergen, and many other places. There are great hippopotamus beds in Sicily, amphibian beds in Texas, mastodons in Florida, horse beds in France, and, of course, beds of shells and other remains of marine invertebrates found practically everywhere. Fossils of insects abound in Colorado, the Baltic nations, the

Caribbean islands, and elsewhere. The vast coal beds are simply fossilized remains of plants.

Then, there are the amazing elephant (or "mammoth") beds of Siberia and Alaska. Literally millions of these huge animals have been entombed in the permafrost soils of the Arctic, occasionally even with the flesh still intact. Also in the permafrost have been found the fossils of many other great mammals—the rhinoceros, camel, horse, and more. All these animals are now found in a region that would be utterly incapable of supporting them today. When they were suddenly buried by fast-moving sediments, they were evidently then living in a warm environment with abundant vegetation. The sudden flood that engulfed and buried them was evidently followed by a rapid change in climate, the temperature in some exposed areas dropping so quickly that certain animals were frozen whole before their flesh could decay. Within months or years, all the soil water likewise had frozen, and the "permafrost" has preserved the fossils of these millions of large animals ever since. Whether these animals were buried by the Noahic flood or by a later regional flood is open to further study, but there is no question that they are evidence for extensive catastrophism.

These Arctic fossils illustrate a remarkable fact evident also in many other geologic data. At one time in earth history there was a worldwide temperate climate. The remains of coral reefs formed by sea creatures that can live only in warm waters have been found so far north that they may underlie the very poles themselves. Coal beds and tropical fossil animals have been found in Antarctica also. Tropical animals have also been found as fossils in Greenland, Spitzbergen, and in practically every other region of the world. Fossil ferns and other tropical and temperate-zone plants have also been found in abundance in the polar regions. Uniformitarian geologists have never been able to explain the worldwide warm climate, which actually eems to be indicated in practically every "age" in the geologic column, nor have they been able to explain the "Ice Age" in the most recent portion of the column, the Pleistocene epoch.

MANY CATASTROPHES OR ONE CATACLYSM?

The remaining question is whether modern neo-catastrophists are right in attributing the geological strata and fossil graveyards to a multitude of local catastrophes separated from each other by millions of years of geological quiescence, or whether the many local catastrophes were all interconnected and essentially contemporaneous, constituting a single worldwide cataclysm. As already shown, the Word of God clearly and unequivocally teaches the latter.

Geological evidence supporting the biblical record includes the fact that the same basic lithology, petrology, mineralogy, and other physical features characterize all the so-called geological ages alike. One would think that the physical aspects of the globe would evolve along with the biological if evolution were really true, but they have not.

Even the fossil evidence is doubtful. As already noted, the actual fossil sequences can be explained adequately even on the basis of a purely random distribution showing no clear "vector of progress" at all, as more and more evolutionists are being forced to admit. Such order as does exist can be explained just as well in terms of ecological zones. There is no intrinsic reason (apart from evolutionary presuppositions) that all the animals and plants now found in the fossils could not actually have been living simultaneously in the pre-Flood world and thus have been buried more or less contemporaneously in the sediments of the Flood.

But the clinching evidence is the fact that, as every geologist must know and agree, there is *no worldwide unconformity* in the worldwide geologic column. An unconformity is a surface between two geological formations, an interface on which erosion has taken place between the two periods of sediment deposition represented by the strata below and above that interface. Such an unconformity may be recognized by a sudden change in the characteristics of the strata, either a change in rock type, fossil contents, or most commonly and importantly, a change in the slope of the strata (i.e., "layers") comprising the two formations.

An unconformity surface typically is formed when an uplift raises the local sediments above the water level, so that deposition on the surface stops and erosion begins. Thus, an unconformity means a time gap in the deposition process. However, although there exist many local unconformities in local geologic columns, it is now known that there is no worldwide unconformity, except at the very bottom of the column.

This can only mean that there were no worldwide time gaps in the processes of deposition that formed the sedimentary rocks, so that the entire geologic column is continuous from bottom to top. If this fact is combined with the now-acknowledged fact that every unit in the column was formed rapidly and catastrophically, it follows that the entire worldwide sedimentary column was formed rapidly and contemporaneously, exactly as in the Noahic Flood recorded in the Bible.

There are many other geological evidences of worldwide hydraulic catastrophisim (clastic dikes, great folds that must have been formed when the sediments were soft, extensive beds of mixed gravels and boulders, ubiquitous "pillows" in the lava rocks of the geologic column, and many more.) Still further evidence is provided by the universal occurrence of evidences of former higher water levels in the rivers and lakes of the world, reflecting the post-Flood period of heavy run-off as the lands were being uplifted and the ocean basins opened up to receive the drainage from the floodwaters (note Psalm 104:6–9). Every inland lake exhibits ancient beaches high on the surrounding hills, and every river reveals old river terraces high above the present flood plains. Furthermore, practically every river is now what is called an "underfit stream," far too small to have produced its own canyon and valley sections or the extensive beds of alluvium through which it flows. All the deserts of the world were, in the recent past, well-watered. All of that has been explained as a pluvial period in the earth's lower latitudes, occurring at the same time as the famous Ice Age in the upper latitudes.

Glacial geologists have never been able to determine the cause of the Ice Age or the accompanying pluvial period for the simple reason that they have refused to recognize the reality of the universal Noahic deluge, which provides a perfect explanation for both. The tremendous impact of the Flood on earth's climatic regime, which earlier had been beautiful and subtropical everywhere, all year long, is more than adequate to explain the Ice Age (lasting perhaps a thousand years after the Flood, not two or three million years, as claimed by uniformitarian geologists) and all other types of "residual catastrophism" in the earth, persisting even to the present day.

Finally, the very fact that practically all of the earth's crust consists of sediments or sedimentary rocks and that these rocks were obviously laid down under moving water (except for the few formed by ice and wind *after* the sedimentaries) is *prima facie* evidence that the entire surface of the earth has, indeed, been under water fairly recently. The geologist may prefer to explain this in terms of differential uplifts at various times, but the fact is that 70 percent of the earth is *still* under water, and even the highest mountain ranges of the world are known to have been uplifted in the recent geological past.

THE CAUSE OF THE FLOOD

There have been many speculative suggestions as to what might have caused the Flood, but it would be wise to limit ourselves strictly to the direct implications of the simple biblical statement on this matter: "In the six hundredth year of Noah's life, in the second month, on the seventeenth day of the month, the same day were all the fountains of the great deep broken up, and the windows of heaven were opened. And the rain was upon the earth forty days and forty nights'' (Genesis 7:11–12). Thus the Flood was caused by a uniquely cataclysmic dual phenomenon: (1) An essentially simultaneous subterranean and submarine eruption of sub-crustal waters all over the world and (2) an immediately following universal torrential downpouring of waters from the skies, continuing unabated for forty days and nights.

Such a cataclysm would be impossible under the present lithospheric and atmospheric regime, and God in fact promised Noah it would never happen again (Genesis 9:8–17). This fact compels us to recognize that the original "very good" world that God created (Genesis 1:31) was vastly different from this present world.

According to Genesis 2:5–6, there was no rainfall, such as we know now, in the antediluvian world, although there were rivers (Genesis 2:10–14) with a subterranean source, evidently emerging from pressurized reservoirs below the earth's crust through controlled springs, perhaps the "fountains of the great deep." Also, since the rainbow was only set in the sky by God after the Flood, any atmospheric water must have been in the vapor state (a rainbow can only be formed by liquid water droplets).

The reference in Genesis 1:6–8 to the "waters which were above the firmament" implies a great body of invisible water vapor (not clouds, which are composed of liquid droplets) above the lower atmosphere. The Hebrew word for "firmament" literally means "expanse" or "stretched-out" thinness or "space." Certain unusual atmospheric conditions may also be indicated by the extreme longevity of the antediluvians, as well as the large sizes of so many ancient animals now found as fossils.

In the present atmosphere, the water vapor would be sufficient to produce a worldwide rain of less than two inches, certainly not enough to sustain global torrents lasting forty days. However, there is enough water in the present oceans to cover the entire earth to a depth of over 1.5 miles, if the terrestrial topography were smoothed to a common elevation. Thus, much of the earth's present oceanic waters must originally have been stored in a vast canopy of water vapor above the earth's atmosphere, extending far out into space as a great protective blanket for the beautiful earth originally created by God as the home for man and animal.

Such a vapor canopy would have resulted in exactly the physical phenomena that both Scripture and the geological record indicate must have prevailed before the Flood. It would have been invisible but would have filtered out most of the cosmic and short-wave-length radiations that now reach the earth. In fact, the small vapor blanket that exists in our present atmosphere is the very thing that makes life possible on the earth today. If these radiations were not at least partially screened out before reaching the earth, they would quickly destroy all life.

The canopy would also have produced a much stronger "greenhouse effect" than now exists, preventing extremes of heat and cold and resulting in a uniformly warm, probably subtropical climate all over the earth. As already noted, the fossil-bearing sedimentary rocks imply that this type of climatic regime prevailed in almost all the so-called geological ages.

The essentially uniform warm temperatures together with the earth's much gentler primeval topography would have caused much different meteorological conditions. Winds and storms would have been impossible, since they result basically from temperature differences. Similarly, the great global atmospheric air mass movements that sustain the present hydrological cycle would have been impossible, and heavy rains could never have occurred, as mentioned in Genesis 2:5. However, as this verse also mentions, there would have been—by daily local evaporation and transpiration, with evening cooling and condensation—a daily mist that would have kept the earth everywhere in a comfortable state of humidity and provided ample moisture (together with the artesian-spring-fed rivers and water table) to sustain lush vegetation and abundant animal life everywhere. The warm waters of the narrow, shallow network of "seas" everywhere (Genesis 1:10) would likewise have sustained a thriving complex of marine life all over the world. The world, indeed, was "very good" (Genesis 1:31) as God originally created it.

Furthermore, it is well known that biological mutations are caused in large degree by radiation. Genetic mutations cause deterioration in future generations of the biological kinds that experience them (thus accounting for decreases in size, viability, and even extinctions of many animals), whereas somatic mutations (in the body cells) cause deterioration and eventual death of the individual creatures experiencing them. These somatic mutations may thus be directly related to longevity. The radiation-free environment of the antediluvian world may have been at least one factor contributing to the long lives of the antediluvian patriarchs and the large sizes of the antediluvian animals.

All of these considerations help us to realize better something of the overwhelming nature of the Flood cataclysm, when all the earth's previously controlled fountains of the great deep "cleaved open" and the vast waters above the firmament suddenly condensed and poured forth from the "floodgates" or "sluiceways" of the heavens. Every square foot of the earth's surface must have been profoundly altered. All creatures, except some of those at home in water and all of those preserved by God in the ark, must have perished, many being buried alive in the sediments.

When Noah and his family came out of the ark a year later, they saw a tremendously different world. No blanket of vapor filtered and diffused the sun's rays any longer and the rainbow appeared in the sky, assuring them that such a flood would never occur again.

The Scriptures do not say whether or not there was some antecedent physical cause that triggered the bursting of the crust and the precipitation of the canopy. Many speculations have been offered, but there is no way to test any of them (approach of an asteroid, tilting of the earth's axis, meteorite bombardment, and so on), so it is best not to advocate any of them dogmatically. When the fountains broke open, the explosive eruption of dust into the atmosphere with the accompanying violent updrafts would be adequate in itself to cause the condensation and precipitation of the canopy. In any case, whatever may have been the detailed sequence of causes and effects, the biblical Flood was a devastating worldwide cataclysm that provides a fully adequate framework within which to explain the known data of geology and paleontology.

OTHER EVIDENCES OF THE FLOOD

The testimony of the Flood has been preserved not only in the rocks and fossils but also in the history and traditions of the entire human race. Practically every ancient nation and tribe in the world has its own flood story, many of them amazingly similar to the biblical account—even in such details as the sending of the dove and the raven to search for land and the offering of sacrifices when the waters subsided. The similarities are not such as to permit the idea, however, that the Genesis account had somehow penetrated to all these scattered regions. Most of the stories have been grossly distorted and exaggerated, with many impossible fancies appended to them. At the same time, it is obvious that they all must have stemmed originally from the same primeval source. That source could only have been the historical event of the Flood and Noah's Ark, with the true and complete record now preserved only in the Bible.

The very peoples and population of the world provide a

convincing testimony to their origin from a common stock at about the time and place indicated in the biblical records. Despite the misleading speculations of the paleoanthropologists, real archaeological evidence almost invariably points to the origin of true civilization (as evidenced by agriculture, animal domestication, pottery, metallurgy, urbanization, and writing) as having occurred somewhere in the Middle East near the eastern shores of the Mediterranean several thousand years ago. The ancient sites in Egypt, Iraq, Crete, Syria, and Turkey all focus on the same general area and time as the true cradle of civilization.

It is bound to be providential that the geographical center of all the land areas of the earth turns out to be near Mount Ararat, the point from which all nations and land animals originally migrated.

Furthermore, the present human population of the world supports the Genesis record. The world population in 1800 has been estimated at about 850,000,000, whereas in 1650 it was only about 400,000,000. In 1986 it was somewhat over 4,000,000,000. The population thus seems to be doubling itself about every one hundred years, and there is no objective reason to assume this rate was significantly lower in the past. The present rate seems to be more rapid than this, in fact.

Now if the original population was two (say Noah and his wife), one can easily calculate that the population would only have to double itself thirty-one times to produce the present world population. Assuming the Ussher chronology to be correct, Noah and his wife had their family about 4,500 years ago. This gives an averaging doubling interval of 145 years, which is quite reasonable and conservative.

However, if the original pair lived, say, five hundred thousand years ago, which is much less than the usual anthropological estimate, the average doubling time is over sixteen thousand years, which is absurd. The world's present population, as well as their dispersal from Ararat (and later Babel), can easily be explained in terms of the biblical framework. The same applies to animal populations and their geographical distribution. During the Ice Age following the Flood, extensive land bridges existed across the Bering Straits and down the Malaysian archipelago into New Guinea and possibly to Australia. People and animals could have migrated on foot to practically all parts of the world. Men also knew how to construct ships, as is evidenced by the Ark itself, and there is increasing evidence of ancient navigation to all regions of the globe, even to Antarctica.

Some people have ridiculed the story of Noah's ark, alleging it would have been impossible for him to keep two of every kind of animal on the ark for a year, but this objection is easily answered. The ark's dimensions are given as 300 cubits by 50 cubits by 30 cubits. Assuming each cubit to be 18 inches (the most likely value, according to archaeologists), each of the ark's three decks (averaging 15 feet in height) would have contained about 34,000 square feet of floor space, and the total carrying capacity of the ark was about 1,500,000 cubic feet, the equivalent of 569 standard railroad stock cars.

The smaller animals were, no doubt, placed in tiers of cages on top of each other, with the few large animals, (e.g., elephants, dinosaurs) in separate stalls. There are (according to leading taxonomist Ernst Mayr) less than 20,000 species of land animals (mammals, reptiles, birds, amphibians) living today, with a much smaller number of extinct species known from the fossils. At the most, therefore, the ark would only have to carry, say, 80,000 animals. If the average animal was the size of a sheep (most animals are much smaller than this), and knowing that a railroad stock car can carry 240 sheep, it is clear that the ark *could* have held as many as 140,000 animals. The biblical "kind" is very likely much broader than the species in most cases, so there would have been no problem at all, in accommodating all the world's land animals in the ark.

They were, no doubt, all young animals (they had to live a

year in the ark, then repopulate the earth) and therefore relatively small and docile. Furthermore, it is likely that many or
most of the animals spent most of the Flood year in a state of
relative dormancy, thus requiring a minimum of care. It is also
noteworthy that Noah did not have to go out and bring them to
the ark. The record says that God caused them to migrate to the
ark as the time for the Flood drew near.

THE AGE OF THE EARTH

Since geologists maintain that the earth is 4.6 billion years
old, in contrast to the biblical record of special creation about
6,000 years ago and the worldwide flood about 4,400 years ago
(assuming a literal six-day creation and no gaps in the genealo-
gies of Genesis 5 and 11), we do need to consider in this
chapter the question of these contradictory dates. The treatment
here must necessarily be simplified for the sake of brevity and
clarity, so it is suggested that any who want a fuller analysis of
this important subject should consult the appropriate references
in the Bibliography.

Although most people today have been conditioned to believe that the earth is very old, it is helpful to keep this theory in
proper perspective. The only histories (i.e., written records) go
back about four thousand years—not 5 million or 5 billion.
Thus, anything beyond four thousand years must involve much
speculation and a number of unverifiable assumptions.

Furthermore, we have already shown that the geologic
column, ostensibly revealing the vast evolutionary ages of geology, actually is the record of just one event—the Flood. It does
not represent the billions of years of the evolution of life over
many ages but the cataclysmic destruction of life in one age.

Where, then, do these imaginary billions of years come
from? Other than the necessity for vast time spans to justify
belief in evolution they are now based mostly on three radiometric
dating methods—uranium/lead, potassium/argon, and rubidium/

strontium. In each case, a "parent" element is supposed to decay into its "daughter" element at a known, very slow rate, so that the amounts of the two now found together in a mineral in a rock will yield the "age" of that rock.

It should be obvious that many unprovable and unreasonable assumptions are involved in such methods, the most unwarranted of which is the assumption that none of the daughter element was already present in the mineral when the latter was formed (e.g., radiogenic lead in the uranium mineral). Practically all such minerals *do* have significant quantities of the daughter product present, however, when the magma in which they are crystallized first cools after flowing up from the earth's mantle. This is practically always true even for minerals in lava rocks newly formed through modern volcanoes. In such cases, the apparent age based on a uranium/lead calculation might well be, say, a billion years even when the rock has just been formed. Since all such radiometric ages are based on minerals like this, solely in igneous rocks, and since these presumably were formed in the same way as modern volcanic rocks are formed, by the flow of a magma from the earth's mantle up through the earth's crust, it is all but certain that all such apparent ages will be immensely greater than the true age of the rock.

Thus, by ignoring the possibility of creation (that is, of God's creating mineral assemblages with parent and daughter elements together to start with), evolutionists can "officially" declare rocks to be billions of years old. But such ages are worthless because they are based on the very assumption they hope to prove—namely, that there was no supernatural creation to begin with.

It is also significant that there are scores of other worldwide physical processes by which one can calculate the age of the earth, and none of those will give anywhere near the billion-year age deduced from these three specially approved radiometric methods.

For example, the rate of decay of the earth's magnetic field will yield a maximum age for the earth of about ten thousand years. So will the worldwide build-up of radiocarbon in the earth's atmosphere and biosphere. The net influx of uranium into the world's oceans, even assuming there was none there to begin with, indicates a maximum possible age of about a million years. The rate at which the sun seems to be shrinking also indicates an age of no more than a million years. The influx of meteoric dust on the earth from space indicates an age too young, even to measure. In my book *The Biblical Basis for Modern Science* (Baker, 1985, pp. 477–80) are listed over sixty worldwide processes like those that indicate an age for the earth (and even the universe) far less than the billions of years demanded by evolutionists.

All such processes that go back beyond the beginning of recorded history (say, five thousand years or so) necessarily involve assumptions that cannot be tested. But the assumptions that lead to a young earth are far more reasonable and conservative than the assumptions on which uranium dating and other such radiometric methods are based. And the numbers of processes that yield a young age exceed by far the very few processes favored by evolutionists because they yield an old age.

Thus the weight of the physical evidence confirms the geological testimony of the Flood. The earth is young, just as the Bible says. It does not even "look old" as evolutionists claim but has only been alleged by them to look old on the basis of the arbitrary and unreasonable assumption of uniformitarianism.

The only way we can know the age of the earth, of course, is for God to reveal it to us. He *has* said, in words inscribed by God's own hand on the stone tablets of His law: "In six days the Lord made heaven and earth, and on the seventh day He rested, and was refreshed" (Exodus 31:17).

4

The Bible and Ancient History

Many sciences have been developed to try to work out the detailed facts of ancient history. These would include such fields as cultural anthropology, archaeology, ethnology, and linguistics; and these have, indeed, thrown much light on ancient cultures and civilizations.

In reference to the Bible, these sciences deal especially with the events of the post-Flood period. As shown in the preceding chapter, the Flood was such a devastating cataclysm that practically all vestiges of any pre-Flood peoples were obliterated. However, there are many recollections of the Flood and the antediluvian world that have been partially preserved in the form of the ancient legends of post-Flood peoples.

ARCHAEOLOGY AND THE BIBLE

It was formerly the all-but-universal custom of Bible critics to attack almost everything mentioned in the Bible as nonhistorical, written long after the events described and, in many cases, simply fabricated by biblical writers. Since the multitude of archaeological discoveries in the past century, however, that has begun to change. The Bible is now regarded by knowledgeable archaeologists and ethnologists, even by those who do not believe in its inspiration, as an exceedingly trustworthy book in matters of post-Abrahamic—even post-Babel—history. The earliest known civilizations of the world were those of Sumeria, Egypt, Babylonia, Syria, Assyria, Persia, and other countries in the region near the eastern shores of the Mediterranean. Many discoveries in these lands bear directly on the historicity of the Bible.

A number of the tablets excavated in the Middle East do, indeed, contain inscriptions dealing with the creation and the world before the Flood. Although there are significant differences in these as compared with the straightforward biblical narrative of this period, they do bear many striking similarities to the Genesis records. Since these tablets in many instances have been dated prior to Moses' time, critics tend to claim that Moses himself got the stories from them, and that, therefore, the Genesis narratives are also mere legends.

However, even a superficial comparison of the majestic accounts in the Bible with the garbled mythologies of these other stories is sufficient to show that the Bible is incomparably superior to them. It is natural to expect that some recollection of the great events of creation, the Fall, the antediluvian patriarchs, the Flood, and the tower of Babel would be handed down by word of mouth to the descendants of Adam and Noah, and it is significant that these ancient tales do show enough resemblance to the Bible accounts to indicate a common ancestral source. That original source, however, was the true account in the Bible, not the distorted accounts of the ancient legends. Much sound evidence indicates that the ancient patriarchs (Adam, Noah, Shem, and so on) all wrote down—as eyewitnesses—the events of their own times. These primeval tablets were handed down through the patriarchal line until they finally came to Moses, who then compiled and edited them into our present book of Genesis.

POST-FLOOD MIGRATIONS

We have already noted the scores of Flood stories throughout the world, in addition to the tremendous geological evidences of the Flood. However, certain archaeological claims of a "flood layer" in Ur and Kish must be understood as recording only a local flood in the Tigris-Euphrates region, not the worldwide Flood of Noah. By the same token, *all* archaeological excavation sites revealing artifacts of early men must be regarded as post-Flood. The Flood was so cataclysmic as to destroy all pre-Flood settlements. Any artifacts remaining from those ancient civilizations would now be buried deep in the geological strata—not at the level of archaeological digs—and, whenever found today, as some have been, they are usually ignored or explained away, since they don't fit in with the concept of geological ages.

The story of the confusion of tongues and dispersion of the peoples at the tower of Babel is commonly ridiculed by skeptics, but there is certainly no better explanation for the origin of the different families of languages. Even the later fractionation of these basic language families into the thousands of languages and dialects of the peoples of the world is still entirely mysterious. Evolutionists have no answer to the question of the origin of human language itself, not to mention the different languages.

Furthermore, it is possible that part of the original tower of Babel is still standing. What seems to have been the greatest of the ancient Babylonian ziggurats was excavated a number of years ago. This tower was already old during Babylon's heyday and had, in fact, been repaired and restored for use in her sacrificial worship ceremonies. The Greek historian, Herodotus, about 500 B.C., described the structure, which then consisted of a series of eight ascending towers, each one recessed in turn, with a spiral roadway running around it as a means of climbing to the top. At the very top, there was probably a great temple emblazoned with the signs of the zodiac and used in the worship

of Babylon's gods. Babylonian legend asserted that it had originally been built by Nimrod, which coincides with the Bible
record. In fact, the region, about ten miles southwest of Babylon's center, is still called *Birs nimroud*. The structure as Herodotus described it was more than seven hundred feet tall, of
which about three hundred feet still remain. If this tower is not
the original tower of Babel, it probably was at least meant to be
a replica of it. In fact, the tower of Babel was probably the
prototype for all the world's ancient ziggurats, pyramids, and
other "high places."

The list of primeval nations in Genesis 10 (also called the
Table of Nations) is by far the most complete and accurate
listing of the tribes and nations of antiquity. One of the world's
greatest archaeologists, William F. Albright, called it "an as-
tonishingly accurate document." It lists the descendants of Shem,
Ham, and Japheth (the three sons of Noah) and indicates the
regions in which they settled and the nations that developed
from those first tribal settlements.

THE TIMES OF ABRAHAM

Direct archaeological evidence of Abraham, Isaac, and the
other early patriarchs of Israel has not yet been found, since
Israel was not yet an organized nation. On the other hand, there
is much collateral evidence illustrating the times in which they
lived, proving that the descriptions of the city-states, the peoples, and the general conditions of life during those times as
given in the Bible is quite accurate and must have been written
by trustworthy eyewitnesses.

For example, Abraham's original homeland is mentioned in
the Bible as Ur of the Chaldees. The very existence of that city
was once doubted by the critics, but it has long since been
excavated and explored. Those numerous critics (many still
holding forth in liberal seminaries) who claimed that the art of
writing was unknown in Moses' day (hence he could not have

written the Pentateuch) were proved wrong when great libraries of tablets at Ur and other places revealed beyond question that practically everyone could write long before the birth of Abraham, let alone Moses.

Further, the theories of those same critics about the gradual evolution of culture, science, and religion have been largely demolished by archaeology. Over and over again, excavations at these ancient cities have revealed that the more recent habitations on those sites were degenerate remnants of earlier, higher civilizations there. There is even much evidence—not only in the Middle East but also all over the world—that the original religions of the earliest settlers recognized the existence of a "high god," but that their primeval monotheism soon degenerated into pantheism, polytheism, and animism.

Discoveries beginning in 1964 in northern Syria have been particularly significant in illuminating the book of Genesis. Over seventeen thousand tablets—in addition to artifacts of many kinds—have been excavated at the site of ancient Ebla. The tablets contain hundreds of geographic names, historical references, allusions to economic matters, and descriptions of religious and judicial practices, including an elaborate code of laws. All of them date prior to the destruction of Ebla by the Akkadians around 2250 B.C. (about two hundred years before Abraham).

The language of the tablets is a Semitic language closely akin to Hebrew. A number of personal names found in the Ebla tablets are clearly equivalent to various names in the book of Genesis (though not the same individuals), including Esau, David, Saul, and Ishmael. The greatest king of Ebla was a man named in the tablets as Ebrum, and this might well be the same man as Eber (Genesis 10:21, 24, 25; 11:14–17), the man from whom the name *Hebrews* was derived. Many Canaanite and Syrian cities familiar in the Old Testament are mentioned in the Ebla tablets. A creation tablet found there is more similar to the Genesis creation record than any others yet discovered.

The invasion of Canaan by the northern confederacy at the time of Abraham (as described in Genesis 14), and probably also the destruction of Sodom and Gomorrah, has been confirmed by recent archaeological excavations. The raining of fire and brimstone (sulphur) from the sky, with the land "smoking like a furnace" could well have been a combined volcanic eruption and earthquake, accompanied by the burning of asphalt and great seeps of natural gas all over the plain. The region near the southern shores of the Dead Sea does give much evidence of some such holocaust in the past.

It has been assumed for a long time that the ruins of Sodom and Gomorrah lie beneath the southern end of the Dead Sea. More recent excavations have revealed the remains of five "cities of the plain" (apparently Sodom, Gomorrah, Zoar, Admah, and Zeboim) overlooking five streams emptying into the eastern shores of this southern leg of the Dead Sea. Burial grounds found near these cities indicate that they were large and prosperous, but (except for Zoar, where Lot remained for a while) they ceased to exist during the time of Abraham.

As far as Lot's wife's turning into salt is concerned (Genesis 19:26), it is likely that she lagged behind (the probable implication of "looked back") and was overcome in the catastrophe. There are huge salt formations in the region, and it may be that she was buried by a mass of salt thrown into the air. It is also possible that she was buried in the lava and ash fall, gradually becoming petrified into "salt" by normal chemical replacement processes through the succeeding years, such as happened to many of the inhabitants of Pompeii and Herculaneum when those cities were destroyed by a volcanic eruption.

THE HISTORY OF ISRAEL

The Hebrew captivity in Egypt and the subsequent Exodus are now almost universally accepted as historical, even by Bible critics. Although no unequivocal evidence of the ten plagues has been discovered, an indirect confirmation has been attained with the archaeological recognition that every one of them seemed particularly aimed at some aspect of the religion of the Egyptians. The deities of the Nile, the goddesses of the frog, the fly, and the cattle, the gods of medicine, the elements, the sun, the fertility of the fields, and finally, the goddess of birth, all suffered tremendous loss of prestige in the minds of the extremely polytheistic Egyptians because of the plagues of Jehovah. Archaeology, by revealing the religion of the Egyptians of Moses' day, indirectly substantiates the biblical records and if possible, gives them even greater meaning.

Some recent writers (Immanuel Velikovsky, Donovan Courville, and others) have pointed out that a reduction of the usually cited standard Egyptian chronology by about six hundred to eight hundred years, with an entirely different pharaoh on the Egyptian throne at the time of the Exodus, will yield an actual Egyptian record of these plagues, as well as other corroborations of the biblical accounts. Since this proposed chronological revision has so far not been accepted by most Egyptologists, this particular confirmation of Old Testament history remains somewhat uncertain at this time. It does, however, appear to be supported by good evidence.

The story of the conquest of Jericho as the children of Israel entered the Promised Land may also have been vindicated by archaeology. At one occupation level, possibly corresponding to Joshua's time, the walls of Jericho were found to have literally fallen "down flat" (Joshua 6:20). Furthermore, it was found that the city had been burned at that time rather than looted—again corresponding to the Bible account. Although there is still some disagreement among archaeologists as to whether or not this event corresponds chronologically to the time of Joshua, the more conservative archaeologists are convinced that the evidence is sound.

Among the people encountered in the Promised Land, both by Abraham and by later generations of Israelites, were the

Hittites. There are many references to them in the Bible, but until the closing years of the nineteenth century there was no external evidence that they ever existed. For many years "higher critics" used the Hittite legend as one of their most telling blows against the inspiration of the Scriptures. Archaeological scholarship, however, has now universally recognized that the Hittites constituted one of the most powerful and influential nations of antiquity.

Essentially the same story can be told of Edom and the Edomites. These people, descendants of Jacob's brother, Esau, are frequently mentioned in the Bible but were completely forgotten in secular history until the nineteenth century, when references to them were found in Egyptian and Assyrian monuments. Eventually the splendidly preserved remains of their capital, Petra, the "rock city," were discovered, and Petra has now become one of the main tourist attractions of the Middle East.

Many artifacts of the ancient Canaanite tribes who inhabited the land during those centuries have been recovered, and they help to solve one of the traditional moral problems in the Bible. The Lord's instruction to Joshua and the Israelites to destroy all these Canaanites has long been regarded as inexcusably cruel and unjust. That event, however, must now be viewed in light of the archaeological evidence of their unspeakably vile culture. Archaeology has demonstrated that Canaan had degenerated into an area of unbridled wickedness and cruelty, including child sacrifice and the grossest immoralities, regularly practiced under the guise of religion.

In our world, the idea that God will punish sin is abhorrent to many. The fact remains, however, that God is a holy God and will one day "be revealed from heaven with his mighty angels, in flaming fire taking vengeance on them that know not God, and that obey not the gospel of our Lord Jesus Christ" (2 Thessalonians 1:7–8). The punishment of the Canaanites was merely a token of that coming judgment. In this case, it was also an act of mercy, designed to spare generations yet unborn the terrible contamination and deadly influence of the Canaanite culture. Even the Canaanite children that were slain were possibly better off (many Christians believe that children dying before the "age of accountability" are safe eternally in Christ on the basis of His atoning death, which paid for their innate sin from Adam, and the lack of deliberate sin at their age), while the adults had descended to such depths of idolatry and depravity as to be irreclaimable. Their influence on the people of God was bound to be corrupting in the extreme if they were not completely removed. In fact, history demonstrated that to be so. When Israel failed to carry out God's command to purge the Canaanites from the Promised Land, they eventually became so contaminated with their beliefs and practices that God had to remove *them* from the land as well.

Many discoveries have also thrown light on the periods of the judges, and then the kings, all strongly supporting the historical accuracy of the Old Testament accounts. During the later period of the divided kingdom, the Assyrian Empire was in its ascendancy, and many discoveries in Assyrian archaeology also illumine and confirm the biblical histories. The failure of Sennacherib to take Jerusalem from King Hezekiah in spite of the seeming invincibility of his mighty army is implied in one of the Assyrian cylinders unearthed at the site of the ancient capital of Nineveh. Hezekiah's pool and conduit, constructed during that time probably in anticipation of the coming Assyrian siege, have been found still intact beneath Jerusalem.

These are only a few of the vast number of discoveries made in the past century that confirm the accuracy and authenticity of the Old Testament histories. Nelson Glueck, perhaps the greatest of all archaeologists of the Bible lands, though not a believer in Bible inspiration, maintained that "no archaeological discovery has ever controverted a Biblical reference."

Problems still exist, of course, in the complete harmonization of archaeological material with the Bible, but none are so serious as not to bear real promise of imminent solution through further investigation. It is significant that, in view of the great mass of corroborative evidence on the biblical history of these periods, there exists today not one·unequivocal find of archaeology that proves the Bible to be in error at any point. How could that be so if the Bible were not indeed the Word of God?

THE AUTHENTICITY OF THE OLD TESTAMENT

It has long been one of the chief tenets of liberal criticism that most of the canonical books of the Old Testament were written long after the events they describe by unknown writers other than the traditional authors, and that they consequently contain many anachronisms and errors. There is no objective proof of such a claim, of course, but it is asserted dogmatically as one of the sure results of modern scholarship.

The Pentateuch in particular has been maligned in this manner. Early in the nineteenth century, liberal theologians developed their "documentary hypothesis," according to which these "books of Moses" were not written by Moses at all but were amalgamations of several separate documents written much later: the J, E, P, D documents, standing for "Jehovist," "Elohist," "Priestly," and "Deuteronomist" respectively. They purported to be able to distinguish these source documents by linguistic study of the vocabularies and styles of the different portions of the Pentateuch.

This theory is contradicted both by the New Testament and by all objective evidence, yet is still taught as fact in most seminaries and college religion departments. There are numerous quotations and clear allusions to the Pentateuch in the New Testament, and Christ Himself spoke of Moses as the author on various occasions. Furthermore, the five books of Moses abound with Egyptian words, roots, and phrases, as would be expected in the writings of an author who was "learned in all the wisdom of the Egyptians" (Acts 7:22). What should have been the *coup de grace* to the documentary theory came in 1980 when a computer analysis of the vocabulary of the Pentateuch conducted at the Hebrew University in Jerusalem showed that the five books all must have had the same author.

Actually, as noted before, it is probable that Moses was the editor rather than the original author of Genesis. Since all the events described in Genesis took place before Moses was born and since there is no reason (other than evolutionary bias) to doubt that the early patriarchs could and did keep their own records, it seems certain that Moses must have drawn on those older tablets handed down to him through the line of the great patriarchs of earlier times as he compiled and edited this first book of the Bible. The phrase "these are the generations of" that occurs eleven times in Genesis seems to mark off the original eyewitness narratives written by Adam, Noah, and the other early patriarchs. These quite possibly were first written on stone or clay tablets by the men whose names are thus recorded on the signature inscriptions and handed down through the patriarchal line, preserving the true history of the race from its very beginnings. They were finally acquired by Moses, who made the necessary editorial transitions and additions and who then picked up the record himself in Exodus, Leviticus, Numbers, and Deuteronomy. This explanation of Genesis also accounts for such differences of style and vocabulary as do exist between the different sections of Genesis. As far as the language was concerned, it is reasonable to assume that since Noah and Shem would certainly not have participated in the rebellion at Babel, their own language was not affected by the confusion of tongues, and theirs was the language transmitted down through the line, along with the patriarchal tablets.

As far as the other books of the Pentateuch are concerned, the critical theory is unable to explain why such a large portion of the writings should have focused on details of the Exodus and the wilderness writings. For example, why did the supposed postexilic writers take so much time and space to describe the minutest details of the construction of the Tabernacle in the wilderness and the forms of worship to be used in connection with it? Most such critics claim that the Tabernacle never even existed.

Finally, it is impossible to imagine why whose writers would have gone to such great pains to deceive people by clothing their writings with a spurious antiquity, claiming them to be the works of Moses. How is it possible that no one, down through all the centuries, seems to have had the slightest suspicion that the writings were not genuine works of Moses until the modern higher critics went to work on them? If they were not really what they were represented to be, it seems impossible that they could ever have been accepted in the first place. Their record of the initiation of the detailed rituals, laws, and ordinances, including the institution and continued observance of the Passover, were presented in the books as having been in effect since Moses. None of those could ever have been accepted at any later date if they were not actually in existence at the time and were believed by the people to have been continually in force since Moses initiated them.

DANIEL AND ISAIAH

In a brief work such as this, it is not feasible to discuss in detail all the arguments for and against the traditional authorship and historical accuracy of all the books of the Old Testament. A wealth of literature on this subject is available for the interested student. The traditional view has been more than adequately defended by conservative scholars.

We do need to consider briefly the prophetical books of Daniel and Isaiah, however, since those have been attacked more vigorously than any other Old Testament books except Genesis. Satan, who is of course strongly opposed to God's eternal plan, has directed his main attacks at those books that emphasize the beginning and the ending of this present world—

hence the attacks on Isaiah and Daniel, which contain numerous fulfilled prophecies and even more prophecies still to be fulfilled in the last days. Isaiah also contains numerous references to creation and the Flood. Critics particularly focus their assault on those prophetic sections that have already been fulfilled, which demonstrate the inspiration of the Bible as well as the miracle of fulfilled prophecy. Some of the fulfillments will be discussed in the next chapter, but here we need to be concerned with the authenticity of these two books. If that can be established, there remains no legitimate basis for rejecting any part of the Old Testament as authentic in date, authorship, or content.

The book of Daniel represents itself to have been written by Daniel over a rather long period of years but all during Judah's exile in Babylon. It is written partially in Hebrew and partially in Aramaic, the latter comprising especially those sections addressed to the Babylonians. It contains the names of some Greek musical instruments, attributable to the extensive commerce of the time between Greece and Babylon, but it also contains a number of Sumerian words, from what had almost become a dead language by the time of Nebuchadnezzar, the king of Babylon. Those portions, at least, could hardly have been written at any later time.

Considerable archaeological evidence has been brought to light that indirectly reveals the genuineness of the setting of the book in the Babylon of Nebuchadnezzar and Cyrus. Excavations have unearthed a building with an inscription indicating its use for the instruction of captive princes and nobles in the learning of the Chaldeans. This proves that the gracious treatment received by Daniel and his three friends was not foreign to Babylonian policy, as critics once had claimed.

A huge furnace was also found with inscriptions to the effect that those who refused to worship the Babylonian gods were incinerated therein, thus indicating the factual basis of the story of the three Hebrews in the fiery furnace. A large pit was discovered that was used for feeding men who disobeyed the decrees of the king to wild beasts. An inscription made by Nebuchadnezzar himself seemed to correspond to the story of the king's madness as described by Daniel.

The most serious criticism of Daniel, however, has been with reference to its alleged historical inaccuracies. According to Daniel, the conquest of the city by the Persians took place while Belshazzar was king, whereas secular history said Nabonidus was king and seemed to have no record even of the existence of Belshazzar. Eventually, however, archaeological research proved that at the time of the fall of Babylon, Nabonidus was away from the city and Belshazzar, his son, was acting as regent in his stead. The Bible, in fact, was found to be accurate in full detail.

The existence of Darius the Mede, leader of the victorious Persian army, was also unknown to secular history for a time, but archaeology has also shown that the references to him are quite plausible.

Nevertheless, critics still insist that Daniel's prophecies must have been written much later than the time of the captivity. This position is forced on them by their denial of the reality of miraculous predictive prophecy. In Daniel 11, there is a very remarkable and detailed prophecy of the histories of Persia, Greece, Egypt, Syria, and the Jews down to about 165 B.C. Therefore, critics insist the book must have been written about this date instead of during the exile, about 536 B.C., as it appears to be and was always believed to be by the ancient scribes.

As a matter of fact, however, Daniel's book contains many other remarkable prophecies, including the very date of the first coming of Christ and some that are being fulfilled today. Even if it had been written in 165 B.C., despite all the evidences of its much greater antiquity, it is still a book of marvelously fulfilled prophecies and thus quite beyond the reach of attacks on its divine inspiration. Jesus Christ Himself called Daniel a "prophet"

(Matthew 24:15), citing a particular prophecy of Daniel yet to be fulfilled.

The book of Isaiah also contains many marvelous prophecies that were later fulfilled, especially in its second major division, chapters 40–66. Therefore, liberals have assumed there were two Isaiahs, with the second one writing after the fulfillments had already taken place (for example, the mention of King Cyrus in chapter 45).

There is, of course, an abundance of evidence and testimony against that notion. The New Testament quotes from both divisions of Isaiah, attributing both to the one prophet Isaiah (see Matthew 4:14–16; 12:17–21).

The discovery in 1948 of the Dead Sea Scrolls, including an early copy of the complete book of Isaiah, confirmed that this was one book with one author. That manuscript has been dated at no later than 100 B.C., earlier by many centuries than any other extant Old Testament manuscripts. It is significant that the manuscript is in all important particulars identical to the received text of Isaiah, bearing a striking testimony to the care and accuracy with which the Hebrew scribes copied and transmitted the Scriptures. The few differences that do exist are mostly matters of spelling, and there are no discrepancies of any real significance at all. There is no indication whatever that the scribe regarded the book as being divisible into two parts composed by different authors.

Since the first discovery, many other manuscripts have been found in caves near the Dead Sea, probably deposited there by the pre-Christian sect known as Essenes. Those manuscripts contain most of the Old Testament and are all essentially identical to the Received Text, in spite of the fact that the oldest copies previously available are dated almost one thousand years later than the Dead Sea Scrolls.

It is interesting that three sections of the book of Daniel were found together with the first Isaiah manuscript. They also have been dated at around 100 B.C. and are practically identical to the Received Text.

We have only surveyed the tremendous archaeological evidence bearing on the Old Testament. Many volumes have been written showing that the Old Testament has been and is being vindicated in a most wonderful way by the finds of archaeology. There are still problems in many of the details, but nothing of any significance has come to light that would cause us to question its historical accuracy.

When we turn to the New Testament, the story is the same. Every modern discovery in archaeology, ethnology, linguistics, or other fields seems to confirm more strongly than ever the historical authenticity of the New Testament as well.

THE AUTHENTICITY OF THE NEW TESTAMENT

Although some still allege that Jesus was only a legendary character who never really existed, there is such a mass of evidence to the contrary that no informed person could seriously hold such a position. Numerous inscriptions and papyri have been discovered that either mention His name as the leader and founder of the sect of the Christians or that simply refer to the amazingly rapid growth of that sect. Many of those date from the first or early second centuries, and it is absurd to suppose that they all resulted from the devotion of a group of fanatics to a legendary character.

It is also fair to say (though liberals may disagree) that the books of the New Testament are completely authentic from the standpoint of authorship and antiquity. Liberal theologians formerly taught that many of the books, if not all, were written long after the time of Jesus by unknown authors. The main targets of such criticisms were the four gospels—especially John—and the book of Acts, as well as the book of Revelation. But the evidence shows that criticism to be wrong.

The book of Acts, for example, chronicling the initial

spread of Christianity, was formerly charged with many historical inaccuracies and with reflecting, in general, a much later period of history than the days of the apostles. However, archaeology has completely refuted any such notion. Practically all the cities and towns mentioned in the book of Acts or in the gospels have been located, with the finds at all those places fully vindicating the accounts in the Scriptures. There are still many remains of the architecture of King Herod throughout Palestine, despite the devastation wrought in A.D. 70 throughout the country by the Romans. Well-preserved relics of a synagogue have been preserved at the site of Capernaum, which may very well have been the synagogue at which Jesus occasionally preached. There are, of course, many other sites and structures that are connected by tradition with Jesus and the apostles, but in most cases those are not susceptible to either proof or disproof.

Miniature images of Diana, such as described in Acts, have been unearthed in Grecian cities. The ruins on Mars Hill, from which Paul delivered his famous sermon to the Athenian philosophers (Acts 17), is visited by thousands of tourists annually. Nearby, an altar "to the unknown God" has been discovered (Acts 17:23).

Inscriptions have been found in great abundance throughout the Mediterranean world, some of them containing names of people actually mentioned in the New Testament. Many Roman coins have been found, including the one bearing Ceasar's likeness (Mark 12:15–16). Inscriptions have been found describing the regular Roman census, probably including the very one during which Jesus was born in Bethlehem.

These finds and many others dating from apostolic times show the historical portions of the New Testament are at least authentic in setting and perspective. The same applies to linguistic analysis. The oldest existing New Testament manuscripts were written in a form of Greek unknown to classical literature, with many words formerly ascribed by the critics to some later origin. However, it is known now, from the many papyri inscriptions dating from the first century and earlier, that this peculiar language now known as Koine (or "common") Greek was the universal language of the common people of the Mediterranean world during the time of Christ and the apostles.

The gospel of John, no doubt because of its strong emphasis on creation and on the deity of Jesus Christ as well as His promised return, has been subjected to great attack through the centuries. Modern critics have tried to date its composition at some three or four centuries after Christ, alleging that its peculiar theology belonged to that period rather than the first century. However, many early second-century writers refer to or quote from John's gospel. Evidence shows that it was composed by John himself no later than A.D. 95. A papyrus fragment of a part of John's gospel found in 1935 cannot be dated later than A.D. 150. That is well within the lifetimes of some who actually knew the apostle. Similar papyrus evidence indicating the first-century origin of the other gospels has also come to light.

There is thus no legitimate reason to question the general authenticity of the historical books of the New Testament. They were assuredly written either by the traditional writers or by those who knew them so well that they could faithfully report the original teachings of Christ and the apostles, as well as the historical events concerning the person of Christ and the spread of the early church. In other words, we can have full confidence that the New Testament record of the person and work of Christ and also of the apostles is in all essentials exactly what was believed and taught by those who knew Him and them in the first century. That fact is valid entirely apart from the question of whether or not the New Testament is divinely inspired and inerrant or even whether all the reports are accurate. There can be *no* doubt that the first-century Christians all *believed* them to be accurate and true.

THE RESURRECTION OF CHRIST

One possible question remains: Could all those first Christians have been wrong? Were the gospel writers (or those who first reported the events) mistaken about what they saw and heard? Or could it all have been a gigantic hoax of some kind, planned and perpetrated by the disciples? There is no doubt that Jesus really lived and was a great teacher, but did He really perform the miracles they reported, and was His life really as perfect as they portrayed it?

Those questions have been discussed at length in many volumes, and there is not sufficient space in a small book such as this to attempt a detailed exposition of the life of Christ. There is one key question, however—one all-important event. *Did Jesus really die and rise bodily from the grave three days later?*

In a real sense, all the facts of the gospel records—the virgin birth, the miracles, the transfiguration, the sinless life— stand or fall with the truth or falsity of Jesus' resurrection from the dead. If Jesus really died and rose again, which is the central and foundational belief of all true Christianity, then He must in truth have been God Himself, the Creator and Sovereign of all creation, for no one but God could conquer the enemy death, which has triumphed in the end over all other men.

Well, *did* Jesus of Nazareth rise from the dead? To deny that means to deny on *a priori* grounds the specific testimony of Matthew, Mark, Luke, John, Paul, and Peter, all of whose writings are soundly established in terms of at least general authenticity. Therefore, it is incumbent upon those who would deny the validity of their testimony of His resurrection to come forth with a more compelling explanation as to why those men reported His resurrection and why their report was believed by such multitudes of people if it wasn't really true. So far this has not been done. There have, of course, been various theories put forth, but all have been weak, and none have been generally accepted even by the skeptics.

The descriptions of the resurrection morning and the later appearances of Christ certainly do not have the character of manufactured evidence. The apparent discrepancies in the different accounts (which, however, on closer examination turn out to be complementary rather than contradictory) alone prove that. The different accounts would have all been in obvious agreement with each other if they were products of collusion. The apostle Paul, acknowledged even by his critics to have been a man of great intellect and discernment, states that he was instantaneously changed from a persecutor of Christians to a Christian himself by the sight of the resurrected Christ. In his classic chapter on the evidences for the resurrection (1 Corinthians 15), he reported that more than five hundred people had seen Christ simultaneously after His resurrection, most of whom were still living when Paul wrote and could verify it.

There is no reasonable doubt that Jesus actually was dead when He was placed in Joseph's tomb. He was crucified. A Roman soldier thrust a sword into His side to assure himself that Christ was dead (the whole purpose of the soldiers being there was to verify that those crucified were dead before they were taken down). Blood mixed with water gushed out of His side, probably evidencing a hemorrhage in the heart cavity. He was placed in a tomb, covered from head to foot with the heavy weight of graveclothes and ointments, with a Roman guard set to watch the tomb after it had been sealed with a great stone. It is nonsense to claim He had merely fainted, then recovered consciousness in the tomb, removed all the graveclothes, and in an extremely weakened condition pushed away the great stone, overpowered all the soldiers, and returned to the disciples. Yet it is just such foolishness that unbelievers must propose in order to get away from the testimony of the empty tomb.

It is a fact of history that the tomb *was* empty early the first day of the week following His crucifixion, and the body was not available to His enemies any longer. The Pharisees and Sadducees would certainly have produced the body if they could have done so in order to halt the rapidly growing Christian faith—even many of the priests were becoming Christians. This rapid growth (there were 3,000 converts at Jerusalem on the Day of Pentecost) can only be explained by the fact that those people knew He had been raised from the dead.

The original fabrication of the unbelievers was the story that the Pharisees bribed the Roman soldiers to tell: that the disciples had stolen the body while the soldiers were sleeping on duty (an offense normally punishable by death). If they really *were* sleeping on duty, of course, they could not have seen the disciples stealing the body; so that could never have been a convincing tale.

The change in the disciples is sufficient refutation. Men who a few days before had been weak, vacillating, doubtful, and fearful for their lives, suddenly became bold, powerful, Spirit-filled proclaimers of salvation through faith in the risen Christ. They had nothing to gain and everything to lose from such a wicked deception, if that is what it was. They were persecuted, regarded as fanatics, and most were finally put to death because of what they were preaching. They and their converts had every reason to examine fully and carefully the basis of their faith. The uniform testimony of even the enemies of Christianity down through the centuries has been that the apostles and the thousands of others that have been slain for their faith all died courageously, without recanting to save their lives. Men do not die like that for something they know to be a lie. Charles Colson has pointed out that he and his fellow Watergate conspirators, brilliant and confident as they were, could not keep their conspiracy covered up. How could a group of uneducated, fearful disciples keep their much less believable "fabrication" from being exposed?

The dual witness of the empty tomb and the postresurrection appearances of Christ (on many occasions to different groups and in varied circumstances), supplemented by the change in character of the disciples, the conversion of Paul, the continued observance of baptism, the Lord's Supper, Easter, and Sunday as the day of worship ever since the formation of the early church, and the personal testimonies of millions of Christians through the centuries combine to make the physical resurrection of Jesus Christ the best-attested fact of history.

THE INFLUENCE OF JESUS CHRIST

Although we have been chiefly concerned in this chapter with the reliability of the Bible in the context of ancient history, it is appropriate to conclude it with a summary of Christ's impact on subsequent history. This in itself is evidence of His unique deity, for His influence upon the world has been ennobling and uplifting to a degree surpassing that of all other teachers and philosophers in the world's history.

While it is unfortunately true that certain segments of organized Christianity have been guilty of religious persecution and other acts contrary to biblical standards, it is nevertheless true that the lives of countless men and women have been redeemed through faith in Christ from lives of sin, fear, misery, and despair to lives of peace, holiness, and love. The morality of whole nations has been elevated by the Christian gospel. Schools, hospitals, and benevolent institutions of many kinds for the alleviation of suffering and the advance of knowledge have been by-products of Christianity wherever the gospel has gone. Jesus Christ has been the inspiration and theme for much of the world's greatest literature, art, and music. The unique greatness of our own country for two hundred years is largely because of its foundation upon creationist and biblical principles.

That all this and much more should result merely from the teachings of an obscure Jewish carpenter would be more inconceivable than that He should be, as He claimed, God's only and eternal Son. As a human being, He was born in a stable in a small village, then was reared in another village that was despised even by His own Jewish countrymen, who themselves have been hated and persecuted by most other nations of the world. He had little formal education, no obvious cultural talents, no financial position, and no political stature. He never wrote a book or led an army or held any position in government or industry or education. He taught a small, motley, unpromising group of followers His doctrines and made seemingly strange and impossible assertions and promises. Then, after only three-and-a-half years of such teaching, He died like a common criminal, executed on a Roman cross.

Yet it was such a man as this who made statements and claims that, if He were only a man like other men, immediately must have branded Him as either a preposterous liar or a mad fanatic. For example, He said on one occasion: "I am the light of the world: he that followeth me shall not walk in darkness, but shall have the light of life" (John 8:12).

If any mere man should ever say such a thing, it would immediately be interpreted by most sensible people as colossal conceit or even rank madness, especially if his human circumstances were as unimpressive as those of Jesus. Yet the amazing truth is that for two thousand years this statement from Christ has sounded natural and true and trustworthy and, in fact, has been demonstrated to be a marvelously fulfilled prophecy. For two thousand years He *has* been the light of the world, inspiring all those institutions, individuals, and motives that have most contributed to all that is worthwhile in our present world. Those who have followed Him have *not* walked in darkness but *have* had the light of life, and there are millions who have so testified.

It was also He who said: "Heaven and earth shall pass away, but my words shall not pass away" (Matthew 24:35). What a preposterous, presumptuous, outrageous claim for any man to make. But now, nearing the end of the twentieth century, multitudes are fearing the earth's imminent destruction through nuclear warfare or other means. Biblical signs of the coming end of the age are being fulfilled in increasing frequency. Yet the words of the Lord Jesus Christ have been more widely distributed, read, and believed by more people all over the world than those of anyone who ever lived.

He made many other such claims and promises that would sound impossible, arrogant, and insane coming from anyone else. Yet through the centuries, men have acclaimed Him as the world's greatest teacher and its most perfect man. In the light of all this, what reasonable conclusion is possible but that He is all He claimed to be and can and will fulfill all His marvelous promises to those who believe on Him?

The center of His mission, His teaching, and His gospel was the redemption of man from sin through His own sacrificial death as man's substitute before a holy God. The completion and acceptance of that offering is guaranteed by His bodily resurrection from the dead, which has been declared again and again by men trained in the analysis of evidence to be the best-demonstrated fact in all ancient history.

Finally, the history of the preservation and circulation of the Bible is itself evidence of the providential care of God for His Word. None of the original manuscripts have been preserved, of course. Both those "autographs" and the early copies made from them were quickly worn out from much use. Nevertheless, there are approximately twenty thousand extant hand-copied manuscripts containing part or all of the New Testament and all dating from before the invention of the printing press. That number is much greater than the available manuscripts of any other ancient writing of any kind.

So many copies were made in the early Christian centuries that, despite all efforts, any attempted suppression or corruption of the Scriptures soon became impossible. Neither the fires of persecution nor the attacks of pseudo-intellectual unbelief have prevented the continued transmission of the Bible. Today, parts or all of the Bible have been translated and published in about 1,500 languages, and more copies have been distributed than of any other book ever written. When we read the Bible in any translation reasonably faithful to those ancient Greek and Hebrew manuscripts, we can be as confident as we can of anything in life that we are reading God's Word.

Thus, the Christian is trusting in the living Son of God, whose bodily presence at the right hand of the Father in heaven is affirmed in Scripture, and whose spiritual presence in the believer's heart and life offers further and conclusive attestation to the great fact that Christ is omnipotent Creator, resurrected Savior, and soon-coming King of kings and Lord of lords.

5

Fulfilled Prophecy

An especially powerful type of historical evidence is that of fulfilled prophecy—historical events written down long before they actually happen. Hundreds of prophecies in the Bible have been remarkably fulfilled exactly as foretold but often hundreds of years later. This type of evidence is unique to the Bible and can be explained only by divine inspiration. God, the Creator of time, is outside of time. He is the One who controls the future and, therefore, is the only One who knows the future.

Bible prophecies are not vague and rambling, such as those of Nostradamus and other supposed extrabiblical prophets. Prophecies in the Bible deal with specific places, people, and events, and their fulfillments can be checked by reference to subsequent history.

CITIES IN PROPHECY

For example, consider the prophecy against that great coastal city of antiquity, Tyre of the Phoenicians, center of the immoral cult of Baal worship. The prophecy is found in Ezekiel 26 and first describes the coming capture and destruction of the city by

Nebuchadnezzar in 572 B.C. (vv. 7–11). This was later fulfilled quite literally, as far as the mainland part of the city was concerned. However, Tyre also controlled an island half a mile away, and many of the inhabitants escaped to that island, which continued as an important city for over two centuries more. The particular judgment pronounced in verses 4–5 seemed unfulfilled: "They shall destroy the walls of Tyrus, and break down her towers: I will also scrape her dust from her, and make her like the top of a rock. It shall be a place for the spreading of nets in the midst of the sea." Eventually, however, Alexander the Great finished what Nebuchadnezzar had begun. In his campaign of conquest through the East, the people of Tyre refused to surrender, and he seemed to have no way to reach the island city. Then he devised the plan of building a causeway from the mainland. The Macedonians then literally scraped the dust of the old mainland city and laid her stones and timber and dust in the midst of the water (see v. 12) to build the causeway (note the change from "he" [Nebuchadnezzar] in verse 11 to "they" in verse 12, indicating different conquerors). The causeway was thus built from the remains of the old city and the island city was captured and sacked. Verse 21 says: "I will make thee a terror, and thou shalt be no more: though thou be sought for, yet shalt thou never be found again, saith the Lord God." The mainland city of Tyre, against which the prophecy was directed originally, was never rebuilt. There are not even any ruins or mounds to mark the spot. The causeway and island now form a desolate peninsula used only by fishermen to "spread their nets" for drying. Eventually a new Tyre village was settled nearby (even continuing to the present); however, the new inhabitants were not Phoenicians but Persians and Arabs.

Tyre's sister city, the ancient city of Sidon, only twenty miles north, had the following prophecy uttered against her: "Behold, I am against thee, O Zidon. . . . For I will send into her pestilence, and blood into her streets; and the wounded shall be judged in the midst of her by the sword upon her on every side" (Ezekiel 28:22–23). No fate of extinction was foretold for Sidon, and it has continued as a substantial town through all the intervening centuries. However, it has had one of the bloodiest histories any city ever suffered. Soon after Ezekiel's prophecy, it was captured by the Babylonians. Later over forty thousand died in a rebellion against the Persians; then it was captured by the Greeks under Alexander the Great in 330 B.C. It was the scene of many fierce battles during the Crusades and the various Turkish wars. In modern times it is in Lebanon, only twenty miles south of Beirut, and seems destined to continue its unhappy history indefinitely.

Tyre and Sidon are only examples. Many other cities were the subject of similar prophecies, generally as a result of their contact with God's chosen people, Israel. Most of the ancient cities in that category were exceedingly wicked and idolatrous and either were enemies of Israel or had a decidedly bad influence on her morals and commitment to God. Consequently, God led the ancient prophets to make many predictions of coming judgment on those cities, predictions that have since been fulfilled. Many books have been written expounding those prophecies and their fulfillments, and it is not feasible to discuss others here. However, a few of those cities and the corresponding biblical prophetic references are listed below as a matter of reference:

Thebes, Egypt (the "No" of Scripture; Ezekiel 30:14–16)
Memphis, Egypt (the "Noph" of Scripture; Ezekiel 30:13)
Ashkelon, Philistia (Zechariah 9:5)
Ekron, Philistia (Zephaniah 2:4)
Gaza, Philistia (Zephaniah 2:4)
Bethel (Amos 3:14–15)
Samaria (Micah 1:6–7)
Jericho (Joshua 6:26)
Capernaum, Bethsaida, and Chorazin (Matthew 11:20–23)
Babylon (Isaiah 13:19–22)
Nineveh (Nahum 1:1; 2:8–13; 3:7–19)
Samaria (Micah 1:6)

Those and many other prophecies directed against specific cities have been fulfilled.

PROPHECIES AGAINST WHOLE NATIONS

Many once-great nations have also been the subject of Bible prophecies. For example, Edom (later Idumea) was a strong nation located next to the Israelites in Palestine. The Edomites, as descendants of Esau, were related to the Israelites but were idolatrous and treacherous, frequently warring with the Hebrew nation. Their land was rugged and their capital city, Petra, had a seemingly impregnable position in the rocks of the mountains. It was a rich trade center, and even today its ruined palaces, carved out of the solid rock, are imposing and magnificent. But many Scriptures (Ezekiel 35:3–9; Jeremiah 49:16–18; and so on) predicted its ultimate overthrow. Edom was to be a desolation, and all her inhabitants would disappear.

The fulfillment was long in coming, for Edom and Petra remained prosperous for many centuries after the coming of Christ. No one knows the full story of their decline, but the land has now been desolate for a long time and the Edomites as a people long forgotten, exactly as the prophets foretold.

A similar judgment of extinction was predicted for the nation of Philistia, another idolatrous and warlike opponent of Israel. They lived west of the Israelites on the seacoast and were frequently in conflict with them from the time of Abraham onward. Eventually came the prophecy of destruction: "O Canaan, the land of the Philistines, I will even destroy thee, that there shall be no inhabitant" (Zephaniah 2:5). "The remnant of the Philistines shall perish, saith the Lord God" (Amos 1:8).

Although some remnants of these people and their major cities (Ekron, Ashdod, Gaza, Ashkelon) persisted for over a thousand years, and the Greeks even named the land of Palestine after them, they eventually disappeared forever. Their land is now part of modern Israel, and new cities (e.g., Ashdod, Gaza) have been built near the ancient sites inhabited by Jews and Arabs, but the Philistines themselves with their idols and temples have vanished.

The nation of Egypt, one of the most ancient of all, was not doomed to extinction. Though she was one of the greatest nations of antiquity, the Scriptures foretold her eventual decline, though not her extinction. "It shall be the basest of kingdoms; neither shall it exalt itself any more above the nations; for I will diminish them, that they shall no more rule over the nations" (Ezekiel 29:15).

The present nation of Egypt, repeatedly rebuffed even by the other Arab nations it seeks to lead and with its own native Egyptian population dominated by the Arabs who long ago conquered it, stands today as a living monument to biblical prophecy—"the basest of kingdoms."

Many other prophecies relating to Egypt—its major cities, its industries, its rivers and canals, its rulers, its exploitation by outsiders, and its general impoverishment—have all been fulfilled. There are also numerous predictions concerning other great nations of the ancient world, including Babylonia, Assyria, Ethiopia, Moab, Ammon, Syria and others, and those too have been fulfilled. Entire volumes have been published on the fulfilled prophecies of the Bible.

In view of the recent increase in prominence of the various Arab nations in current world affairs, two ancient prophecies concerning these descendants of Ishmael are of special interest: "And he [Ishmael] will be a wild man [literally, "a wild ass among men"]; his hand will be against every man, and every man's hand against him; and he shall dwell in the presence of all his brethren" (Genesis 16:12). "Behold, I have blessed him [Ishmael], and will make him fruitful, and will multiply him exceedingly" (Genesis 17:20).

THE NATION OF ISRAEL

Of all the ancient nations, however, the nation of Israel figures most prominently in the prophecies. Their entire history has been foretold in the Bible in many prophetic passages. In Deuteronomy 28, even before the Israelites had entered the Promised Land, Moses predicted their future happiness in the land, their repeated sufferings and punishments for disobedience to God's laws, and finally their great worldwide dispersion among the Gentile nations.

This dispersion was also prophesied by many later prophets and finally by Christ Himself (Luke 21:20–24), along with many details of the terrible persecutions that they would suffer in the nations. But it was also revealed that they would not be destroyed or assimilated (as the Edomites and Philistines) and that their national identity would be retained. "Though I make a full end of all nations whither I have scattered there, yet will I not make a full end of thee" (Jeremiah 30:11).

Their eventual restoration as a nation, while still in unbelief, is indicated in many Scriptures. Though it was after "many days," as prophesied in Hosea 3:4, eventually Israel was indeed established as a recognized nation (in 1948) and even regained its ancient capital of Jerusalem in 1967.

THE COURSE OF EMPIRES

The book of Daniel contains some of the most amazing prophecies in the Bible. In chapters 2, 7, 8, and 11 of that book, the entire history of the world is foretold from the time of Nebuchadnezzar to the end. The careers of Babylonia, Medo-Persia, Greece, Egypt, Syria, and Rome are described with such wealth of description and detail that no one acquainted with the facts of ancient history could possibly be uncertain as to the events and nations under discussion. That minuteness of detail is the only crutch of the critical school, which seeks to date the book of Daniel as written after the events under discussion. As pointed out in the preceding chapter, however, the book of Daniel is fully authentic both as to author and date, and thus its marvelous prophecies stand fully vindicated.

Another remarkable prophecy dealing with the world and its nations as a whole is Genesis 9:25–27, accurately outlining the broad future of the three streams of nations coming from Noah's three sons.

MESSIANIC PROPHECIES

Scores of Old Testament prophecies (some expositors have listed more than 300 such prophecies) were fulfilled at the first coming of Christ. At least 90 of those messianic prophecies are specifically mentioned as such in the New Testament. Only a few of the more obvious ones can be listed here. For example:

Virgin birth	Isaiah 7:14	Parted garments	Psalm 22:18
Born in Bethlehem	Micah 5:2	Nakedness	Psalm 22:17
Tribe of Judah	Genesis 49:10	Thirst	Psalm 22:15
Son of David	2 Samuel 7:12–16	Vinegar	Psalm 69:21
Son of God	Psalm 2:6–7	Side pierced	Zechariah 12:10
Triumphal entry	Zechariah 9:9–10	Bones unbroken	Exodus 12:46
Price of betrayal	Zechariah 11:11–12	Sacrifice	Isaiah 53:5–11
Silence at trial	Isaiah 53:7	Finished	Psalm 22:31
Condemned	Isaiah 53:8	Burial	Isaiah 53:9
Crucified	Psalm 22:16	No corruption	Psalm 16:10
Cry on the cross	Psalm 22:1	Three days	Jonah 1:17
Mocking crowd	Psalm 22:6–8	Ascension	Psalm 24:3–10

Of special significance are the two great prophetic chapters describing His suffering, death, and resurrection. Psalm 22, giving a graphic portrayal of His crucifixion, was written by David one thousand years before its fulfillment at a time when execution by crucifixion was practically unheard of. Isaiah 53 presents the most detailed and forceful exposition of the substitutionary, atoning nature of His death of any chapter in either the Old or New Testament. Both chapters conclude with a great note of triumph, implying the completion of His sacrifice and His victory over death.

THE SEVENTY WEEKS

Perhaps the most amazing of all messianic prophecies, however, is Daniel's prophecy of the seventy weeks (Daniel 9:24–26). That prophecy was given to Daniel through the angel Gabriel, revealing the future history of Israel and the exact time of the coming of Messiah. It was given about 538 B.C. while Israel was in captivity in Babylon, with the city of Jerusalem and the holy Temple in ruins. Daniel was told that the prophetic clock would begin again for Israel, as it were, when a command was given to rebuild and fortify Jerusalem. That command was given to Nehemiah by Artaxerxes, king of Persia (Nehemiah 2:5–8) in 445 B.C.

From that date, the prophecy indicated that 483 years (i.e., sixty-nine "weeks" or literally, "sevens," or seven-year periods) would elapse until the coming of Messiah as Prince of Israel. Allowing for errors in our present system of chronology (Jesus was actually born about 4 B.C.) and for probable use of a prophetic year of 360 days instead of an actual solar year, it is obvious that this period culminated at about the time of the public ministry of Christ. In fact, Sir Robert Anderson showed that, with certain reasonable assumptions, its fulfillment may have occurred on *the very day* that Christ for the first time accepted and encouraged His recognition by the people as King of Israel, the day of His so-called "triumphal entry" into

Jerusalem, less than a week before His rejection and crucifixion. Later, weeping over His rejection by His people, He said: "If thou hadst known, even thou, at least in *this thy day,* the things which belong unto thy peace! But now they are hid from thine eyes" (Luke 19:42, emphasis added).

The prophecy also foretold that, after His coming, He would be "cut off" and would "have nothing." That is, He would be rejected as Israel's promised Messiah and executed. This, of course, is exactly what happened. Then, "the people of the prince that shall come" would later "destroy the city and the sanctuary." That was fulfilled when the Romans leveled Jerusalem and its Temple in A.D. 70.

PROPHECIES OF THE LAST DAYS

There are also a great many Bible prophecies whose fulfillments are specifically tied to the "last days"—that is, the times just prior to the second coming of Christ. Many are apparently being fulfilled in our present day. Even though some of those (e.g., "famines and pestilences") have also characterized various other times in history, it is their *contemporaneous* fulfillment that is significant as an evidence of divine inspiration—and also as a sign of the imminent return of the Lord. A few of those modern-day prophecies are listed below.

1. The restoration of Israel to her own ancient land as a recognized nation among nations (Isaiah 11:10–12; Ezekiel 20:34–38; 36:24–25; and so on). This current restoration is not the ultimate fulfillment of these passages but does prepare the way for it.
2. The rise of Russia to world prominence and especially its emergence (with its satellite nations and other communistic states) as a Mediterranean power at the head of a confederacy encircling and attempting to destroy restored Israel (Ezekiel 38:1–23). It can be compellingly shown that "Gog," "Magog," and "chief prince" (literally, "prince of Rosh") in this passage refer to Russia.

3. Rapid increase of science, communication, and travel (Daniel 12:4).
4. Widespread moral and spiritual deterioration, even among religious people (2 Timothy 3:1–7, 12–13).
5. Doctrinal apostasy of religious leaders (1 Timothy 4:1–3; 2 Peter 2:1–2; 2 Timothy 4:3–4).
6. Dominance of evolutionism and uniformitarianism among intellectual leaders, even in Christian nations (2 Peter 3:3–6).
7. Conflicts between capitalistic and laboring classes (James 5:1–8).
8. Preparations for world government, world economic controls, and world religion (Revelation 13:7–16).
9. Widespread materialism and secularism (Luke 17:26–30; 18:8).
10. Intermittent outbreaks of worldwide wars, famines, earthquakes, and diseases (Luke 21:10–11).
11. Rise of socialism and communism (Daniel 2:34–35, 41–43).
12. Fear of the dangerous future coming to the world (Luke 21:25–26).
13. Rise of the nations of the East (Daniel 11:44; Revelation 16:12).
14. Increasing occupation with UFO's and other real or imagined fearful sights in the heavens (Luke 21:11).
15. Revival of occultism and drug use (1 Timothy 4:1; Matthew 24:24; Revelation 9:21; 18:23).
16. Revival of paganism and idolatry (Revelation 9:20; 13:14–15).
17. Worldwide preaching of the gospel (Acts 1:8; Luke 24:47; Matthew 24:14).

This is only a partial list, but enough to make the point. Evidently, as both Scripture and current history clearly teach, world conditions will become increasingly perilous and anti-Christian as the return of the Lord draws near. At the same time, these negative events become positive as we realize that their simultaneous fulfillment further confirms the inspiration and authority of the Bible, as well as the joyful hope of Christ's soon return.

PROPHECY AND MATHEMATICS

It is significant that the validity of this type of evidence (fulfilled prophecies) can be evaluated mathematically using the methods of probability analysis. One can estimate the probability of chance fulfillment of any specific prophecy by determining the number of alternative ways in which the given circumstances might have combined. For example, Jacob's prophecy that Judah would be the progenitor of the Messiah (Genesis 49:10) would have a probability of one out of twelve, since there were twelve tribes from which Messiah might have come. Micah's prediction that Christ would be born in Bethlehem (Micah 5:2) would have a probability, say, of one out of a hundred, on the assumption that there were about a hundred towns and villages in Judah where He might have been born. Then, the combined probability that *both* events could have been predicted by chance would be 1/12 multiplied by 1/100 or 1/1200.

This type of calculation can be extended indefinitely, multiplying individual probabilities together to get the combined probability of all the prophecies being fulfilled by chance in the same individual. When I was still teaching my regular college class in Christian evidences, each student would be assigned as a class exercise a particular messianic prophecy to evaluate, calculating its probability of chance fulfillment. Then, after each paper was checked to see if the analysis was reasonable, all were multiplied together to get the effective probability of all of them put together.

A typical class of students would analyze about twenty separate prophecies in this manner, each prophecy having been fulfilled by Christ at His first coming. The combined probability

in one typical instance turned out to be one chance in 10^{175}.
That number could be written as "1" followed by 175 "0's."

To illustrate the magnitude of such a number, imagine a
universe that is 5 million-billion-billion light-years in radius, all
solidly packed with infinitesimal particles, each of which is only
one-fourth of a millionth of a billionth of an inch in diameter.
The total number of such particles, then, turns out to be 10^{175}.
Now, imagine one particle is painted red, while all the others
are painted white. Stir them up well with a giant paddle, and
then send a blind man into the great sea of particles to pick just
one. The chance that he would select the red particle is the same
as the probability that those twenty prophecies could have all
been fulfilled by chance in the life of one individual.

And that calculation was based on only twenty of the three
hundred messianic prophecies, not to mention all the other
biblical prophecies. There can be no rational reason whatever,
therefore, for anyone of sound mind not to accept the divine
inspiration of the Bible. "For the prophecy came not in old time
by the will of man; but holy men of God spake as they were
moved by the Holy Ghost" (2 Peter 1:21). It could have come
in no other way.

The problem is that "the god of this world [that is, the
devil] hath blinded the minds of them which believe not, lest the
light of the glorious gospel of Christ, who is the image of God,
should shine unto them" (2 Corinthians 4:4).

This glorious gospel of salvation can, however, shine into
the hearts and minds of all who will simply open them up to
Christ by a simple act of the will. We can, of course, only come
to Him by His grace, through personal faith in His saving work
and power. As we have seen in this book, however, that faith is
a *reasonable* faith, based on solid evidence, and it is my prayer
that many readers will choose to come.

Bibliography

CHAPTER 1: SCIENCE IN THE BIBLE

Lockyer, Herbert. *All the Miracles of the Bible* (Grand Rapids: Zondervan, 1961). A thorough exposition of the biblical miracles, both individually and in a general theoretical context.

McMillen, S. I. *None of These Diseases* (Westwood, N.J.: Revell, 1963). A fascinating discussion of the remarkable medical andphysiological insights of the Bible.

Morris, Henry M. *The Biblical Basis for Modern Science* (Grand Rapids: Baker, 1984). The most complete general textbook available on all aspects of the Bible's relation to each important field of science.

————. *King of Creation* (San Diego: Creation-Life, 1980). A cogent treatment of science and Scripture emphasizing Christ as Creator and Sovereign of the world. Foreword by Josh McDowell.

————. *Men of Science—Men of God* (San Diego: Creation-Life, 1982). Brief biographies of sixty-two great Bible-believing scientists of the past, including most of the "founding fathers" of modern science.

————. *Sampling the Psalms* (San Diego: Creation-Life, 1978). Brief exposition of the psalms with unusual scientific insights, as well as those with other special evidences of divine inspiration.

Morton, Jean. *Science in the Bible* (Chicago: Moody, 1978). Beautifully illustrated volume discussing many examples of modern scientific knowledge in the Bible. Written by a Ph.D. biochemist.

Mulfinger, George, ed. *Design and Origins in Astronomy* (Norcross, Ga.: CRS Books, 1984). An anthology of articles on astronomy and the Bible by a number of creationist scientists and theologians.

Rimmer, Harry. *The Harmony of Science and Scripture* (Grand Rapids: Eerdmans, 1976). An updated reprint of an older classic exposition of the scientific reliability of the Bible.

Steidl, Paul B. *The Earth, the Stars and the Bible* (Phillipsburg, N.J.: Presbyterian and Reformed, 1979). An analysis of astronomy in light of biblical revelation written by a Christian astronomer.

Williams, Emmett L., and George Mulfinger. *Physical Science for Christian Schools* (Greenville, S.C.: Bob Jones Univ., 1974). A general textbook on the various physical sciences, with insights and applications from Scripture.

Wood, Nathan H. *The Trinity in the Universe* (Grand Rapids: Kregel, 1978). A classic exposition of the scientific evidence of triunity pervading all aspects of the created cosmos.

CHAPTER 2: THE THEORY OF EVOLUTION

Frair, Wayne, and William P. Davis. *A Case for Creation* (Chicago: Moody, 1983). A brief but effective summary of the major scientific evidences against evolution.

Gish, Duane T. *Evolution: The Challenge of the Fossil Record* (San Diego: Creation-Life, 1985). The most complete scientific critique of the key fossil evidence on the history of life, written by the most experienced scientific debater for creationism. An enlarged version of his best-selling *Evolution—The Fossils Say No!*

Lester, Lane P., and Raymond G. Bohlin. *The Natural Limits to Biological Change* (Grand Rapids: Zondervan, 1984). A sound creationist treatment of biological science in relation to origins.

Moore, John N. *How to Teach Origins Without A.C.L.U. Interference* (Milford, Mich.: Mott Media, 1983). A comprehensive summary of the evidence for scientific creationism, organized in a two-model context by a former Michigan State professor who taught such a course for many years.

Morris, Henry M. *Creation and the Modern Christian* (San Diego: Creation-Life, 1985). A strategic exposition of the foundational importance of creationism to true Christianity, as well as the pervasive harmfulness and unscientific nature of evolution. Foreword by Charles Ryrie.

———. *Evolution in Turmoil* (San Diego: Creation-Life, 1982). A pungent and well-documented treatment of modern evolutionism in its current conflicts and changes, especially as affected by the creationist influence.

———. *History of Modern Creationism* (San Diego: Creation-Life, 1984). The most complete account of the background and significance of the modern creationist revival, as well as of the creation-evolution conflict both in antiquity and in the prophetic future.

———. *Scientific Creationism* (San Diego: Creation-Life, 2d ed., 1985). The book generally regarded as the definitive textbook on modern scientific creationism. Thoroughly documented. Also includes detailed exposition of biblical creationism.

———, and Gary E. Parker. *What Is Creation Science?* (San Diego: Creation-Life, 1982). Modern creationism expounded solely in terms of scientific evidence. Foreword by Dean Kenyon, former leading evolutionary biologist. Well documented and illustrated.

Pinkston, William S., Jr. *Biology for Christian Schools* (Greenville, S.C.: Bob Jones Univ., 1980). A high-school level textbook on biology, written from the perspective of biblical creationism.

Pitman, Michael. *Adam and Evolution* (London: Rider, 1984). An excellent exposition of scientific creationism by a British biologist, published by a secular publishing house.

Sunderland, Luther. *Darwin's Enigma* (San Diego: Creation-Life, 1985). A unique exposition of the case against evolution, based on interviews with leading museum directors.

Taylor, Ian T. *In the Minds of Men: Darwin and the New World Order* (Toronto: TFE Publications, 1984). A comprehensive and convincing critical analysis of evolutionism from both scientific and sociological perspectives.

Thaxton, Charles B., Walter L. Bradley, and Roger L. Olsen. *The Mystery of Life's Origins* (New York: Philosophical Library, 1984). A devastating scientific critique of naturalistic theories of the origin of life by three Ph.D. scientists.

Wilder-Smith, A. E. *The Natural Sciences Know Nothing of Evolution* (San Diego: Creation-Life, 1981). A brief but powerful scientific critique of evolution written by Europe's leading creationist scientist, who holds three earned doctorates in science.

Williams, Emmett L., ed. *Thermodynamics and the Development of Order* (Norcross, Ga.: CRS Books, 1981). A scientific symposium on the key evidence against evolution from the laws of thermodynamics.

CHAPTER 3: SCIENCE AND THE FLOOD

Austin, Steven A. *Catastrophes in Earth History* (El Cajon, Calif.: Institute for Creation Research, 1984). An extensive, well-indexed, annotated bibliography of current books and articles advocating catastrophism from the secular geological literature.

Barnes, Thomas G. *Origin and Destiny of the Earth's Magnetic Field* (El Cajon, Calif.: Institute for Creation Research, 1983). A technical exposition of one of the most conclusive proofs that the earth is young, with answers to objections from critics.

Coffin, Harold. *Origin by Design* (Washington, D.C.: Review and Herald, 1983). An excellent exposition of recent creationism and flood geology by a paleontologist at the Geoscience Research Institute of Loma Linda University.

DeYoung, Donald B., and John C. Whitcomb. *The Moon: Its Creation, Form and Significance* (Winona Lake, Ind.: BMH Books, 1978). Scientific and biblical evidence for the recent origin of the moon by special creation.

Dillow, Joseph C. *The Waters Above* (Chicago: Moody, 1981). A thorough scientific and biblical exposition of the theory of the earth's water vapor canopy before the great Flood.

Howe, George, ed. *Speak to the Earth* (Phillipsburg, N.J.: Presbyterian and Reformed, 1975). An anthology of articles on flood geology and other topics in creationist earth science appearing in the *Creation Research Society Quarterly*.

Morris, Henry M., and John C. Whitcomb. *The Genesis Flood* (Phillipsburg, N.J.: Presbyterian and Reformed, 1961). The book that many believe was the chief catalyst stimulating the modern creationist revival. The most comprehensive treatment of the biblical and scientific implications of the Noahic deluge, with a definitive exposition of Flood geology and recent creationism.

Morris, Henry M. *Science, Scripture and the Young Earth* (El Cajon, Calif.: Institute for Creation Research, 1983). A brief but well-documented answer to the supposedly scientific arguments against the young earth and universal Flood doctrines.

Mulfinger, George, and Donald E. Snyder. *Earth Science for Christian Schools* (Greenville, S.C.: Bob Jones Univ., 1979).

134 Science and the Bible

An excellent creationist textbook on geology and the other earth sciences from the biblical creationist point of view.

Nelson, Byron C. *The Deluge Story in Stone* (Minneapolis: Bethany Fellowship, 1968). The most extensive historical study of flood geology, its displacement by uniformitarianism, and its modern revival. Also an excellent analysis of the world's many flood legends.

Read, John G. *Fossils, Strata and Evolution* (Culver City, Calif.: Scientific Technological Presentations, 1979). Brief, well-illustrated critique of the overthrust concept and other stratigraphic fallacies in evolutionary geology.

Slusher, Harold S. *Age of the Cosmos* (El Cajon, Calif.: Institute for Creation Research, 1980). A technical study of the many evidences from astrophysics and other sciences for the recent creation of the universe.

Whitcomb, John C. *The World That Perished* (Grand Rapids: Baker, 1973). A brief sequel to *The Genesis Flood* by one of its coauthors, with answers to published critical reviews of the book plus additional evidences supporting the biblical record.

CHAPTER 4: THE BIBLE AND ANCIENT HISTORY

Allis, Oswald T. *The Old Testament: Its Claims and Critics* (Phillipsburg, N.J.: Presbyterian and Reformed, 1972). One of the best and most thorough defenses of the authenticity of the Old Testament.

Bruce, F. F. *New Testament Documents: Are They Reliable?* (Grand Rapids: Eerdmans, 1954). Perhaps the best summary of the evidences of the historical authenticity of the New Testament manuscripts.

Courville, Donovan. *The Exodus Problem and Its Ramifications,* 2 vols. (Loma Linda, Calif.: Crest Challenge, 1972). A new system of Egyptian chronology, showing that many key correlations of archaeology with Bible history can be obtained if the standard chronology is reduced by about eight hundred years.

Davis, John J. *Moses and the Gods of Egypt* (Winona Lake, Ind.: BMH Books, 1971). An incisive commentary on the book of Exodus, with special emphasis on archaeological confirmations and insights on ancient Egypt and the Sinai.

Kang, C. H., and Ethel R. Nelson. *The Discovery of Genesis* (St. Louis: Concordia, 1979). A remarkable analysis of Chinese linguistics and ethnology, showing striking correlations with the book of Genesis.

McDowell, Josh. *More Evidence That Demands a Verdict* (San Bernardino, Calif.: Campus Crusade, 1975). An excellent popular critique of the documentary theory of the Old Testament and the so-called "form criticism" of New Testament documents.

――――. *The Resurrection Factor* (San Bernardino, Calif.: Here's Life, 1981). An excellent modern summary of the evidences for the historicity of Christ's bodily resurrection.

Morris, Henry M. *The Genesis Record* (Grand Rapids: Baker, 1976). A verse-by-verse narrative exposition of the book of Genesis, emphasizing its historicity and scientific accuracy, also incorporating relevant insights from archaeology and ethnology.

――――. *Many Infallible Proofs* (San Diego: Creation-Life, 1974). A widely used reference handbook on practical Christian evidences, stressing the Bible's historical authenticity and the many infallible proofs of the deity of Christ.

Pilkey, John. *Origin of the Nations* (San Diego: Creation-Life, 1984). An original and in-depth correlation of ethnological and linguistic data from ancient nations, indicating their common origin and providing new insights on the antediluvian world.

Richardson, Don. *Eternity in Their Hearts* (Ventura, Calif.: Regal, 1981). Fascinating exposition by a missionary scholar, showing the common tradition of primeval special creation

held by remote tribes all over the world, indicating common descent from Noah after the Flood.

Stanton, Mary, and Albert Hyma. *Streams of Civilization* (San
Diego: Creation-Life, 1976). Probably the only modern
textbook on ancient history written in a framework of
creationism and biblical inerrancy and historicity.

Thompson, J. A. *The Bible and Archeology*, 3d ed. (Grand
Rapids: Eerdmans, 1980). Probably the most authoritative
and up-to-date as well as conservative general treatment of
biblical archaeology available.

Wilson, Clifford. *Ebla Tablets: Secrets of a Forgotten City* (San
Diego: Creation-Life, 1977). A popular summary of the
biblical implications of the remarkable recent archaeological discoveries in northern Syria, written by an Australian
archaeologist and psycholinguist.

CHAPTER 5: FULFILLED PROPHECY

Cooke, A. Ernest. *Fulfilled Prophecy* (Chicago: Moody, 1963).
Brief but persuasive exposition of the better-known fulfilled prophecies of the Bible.

Custance, Arthur C. *Noah's Three Sons* (Grand Rapids:
Zondervan, 1975). A thorough exposition of the manifold
fulfillment of Noah's ancient prophecy of the three streams
of nations descending from his sons.

————. *Striking Fulfillments of Prophecy* (Ottawa: Doorway
Papers, 1962). A brief exposition of a number of little-
known fulfilled prophecies in Scripture.

McDowell, Josh. *Evidence That Demands a Verdict* (San Bernardino, Calif.: Campus Crusade, 1972). A major handbook on Christian evidences, with excellent sections on
fulfilled prophecy, probability, and the deity of Christ.

Morris, Henry M. *The Revelation Record* (Wheaton, Ill.: Tyndale, 1983). A verse-by-verse narrative exposition of the
book of Revelation, stressing its literal future historicity

and scientific rationality, showing the close imminence of the return of Christ.

Payne, J. Barton. *Encyclopedia of Biblical Prophecy* (New York: Harper and Row, 1973). Extensive treatment of the significance of prophecy, with analysis of many specific fulfillments in both Old and New Testaments.

Stewart, Herbert. *The Stronghold of Prophecy* (London: Marshall, Morgan and Scott, 1941). One of the most complete and cogent expositions of the Bible's fulfilled prophecies as an evidence of its divine inspiration.

Stoner, Peter B., and Robert C. Newman. *Science Speaks* (Chicago: Moody, 1976). An examination of fulfilled prophecies in terms of probability by a mathematics professor, updated by a scientist-theologian.

Walvoord, John F. *The Nations in Prophecy* (Grand Rapids: Zondervan, 1978). A fine exposition of the prophetic passages dealing with the nations of the Bible, both the fulfilled prophecies of antiquity and those being fulfilled today, written by the former president of Dallas Seminary.

Whitcomb, John C. *Daniel* (Chicago: Moody, 1985). A brief but careful and scholarly exposition of the book of Daniel, with emphasis on its prophetic passages.

Willmington, H. L. *Signs of the Times* (Wheaton, Ill.: Tyndale, 1981). An informative and original exposition of prophecies currently being fulfilled, especially in the moral, religious, and political realms.

Index of Subjects

Index of Persons

Index of Scripture

Moody Press, a ministry of the Moody Bible Institute, is designed for education, evangelization, and edification. If we may assist you in knowing more about Christ and the Christian life, please write us without obligation: Moody Press c/o MLM, Chicago, Illinois 60610.